C. J. (Charles John) Cornish, Charels John Cornish

The Isle of Wight

C. J. (Charles John) Cornish, Charels John Cornish

The Isle of Wight

ISBN/EAN: 9783744724357

Printed in Europe, USA, Canada, Australia, Japan

Cover: Foto ©Thomas Meinert / pixelio.de

More available books at **www.hansebooks.com**

THE

ISLE OF WIGHT

By

C. J. CORNISH

Author of "Wild England of To-day," "The New Forest," &c.

LONDON
SEELEY AND CO. LIMITED, ESSEX STREET, STRAND
NEW YORK, MACMILLAN AND CO.
1895

LIST OF ILLUSTRATIONS

THE ISLE OF WIGHT

CHAPTER I

YARMOUTH AND THE "ISLE OF FRESHWATER"

The "King of the Isle of Wight"—The island a separate region, politically and geographically—Its early "Lords"—Repeated French invasions—Its gallant resistance—Its towns burnt—Their recovery after the fortification of the island by Henry VIII.—How Henry VIII. obtained the money for this—The melancholy history of Yarmouth—Its Castle—Revival of the town—Its present condition—Lord Holmes—The "Isle of Freshwater"—Its coast and cliffs—A visit to the seafowl in the Freshwater cliffs—Totland Bay—Alum Bay—The Needles—Scratchell's Bay—The great precipices—Number of rock-fowl—A cragsman on the cliff face.

WHEN Henry VI., with his own hands, crowned Henry Beauchamp Duke of Warwick, "King of the Isle of Wight," he was not so mad as is commonly believed. For though, as my Lord Coke observed in his *Institutes*, the king has no power to transfer the sovereignty of any part of his dominions, the Isle of Wight seems marked out, both by its position and history, for separate and peculiar consideration. It is the only part of England which has again and again been devastated by foreign invasion. There alone, on British soil, are towns and ports to which the population has never fully returned after their homes were sacked and burned by French and Spanish soldiers. The islanders, on the other hand, have more than once rallied and repulsed their invaders unaided, and for centuries maintained a separate military organisation, which often baffled such attempts at the moment of disembarkation.

Whether held by hereditary petty sovereigns, as it was until the days of Edward I., or governed by wardens and captains nominated by the Crown, the island has always enjoyed in some sort a peculiar form of government, and its recent recognition as a separate county is justified on all grounds, political and historical, as well as geographical. William the Conqueror granted the island to William FitzOsborne, " to be held as freely as he himself held the realm of England." After a brief period of forfeiture, the first of a series of new " lords " was found in the person of Richard de Redvers, Earl of Devon, to whom the island was granted by Henry I., and in whose family it remained until the last of his descendants, the Lady Isabella de Fortibus, Countess of Albemarle and Devon, Lady of the Isle of Wight, and Chamberlain of the Exchequer of England, after the strongest, and as her enemies alleged, the most arbitrary reign of any of her family, was on her deathbed induced to convey the island to Edward I. for the sum of 6,000 marks, a sum computed by Sir R. Worsley, in 1781, to be equal to 60,000 pounds of our money. The resolute countess would not part with her property until she knew herself to be almost *in extremis*, and then voluntarily ordered the deed to be prepared, sent her woman for her great seal, and delivered seisin of the island to the king by handing to the Bishop of Durham, who acted for Edward I., a pair of gloves which she held in her hand. She then signed her will, was shrived by her confessor, and died between midnight and morning.

The unity of " The Wight " was not lost by this change of authority from the " lords " to the Crown. Constant reprisals by French fleets for English invasions, levies *en masse* of the islanders under their wardens or captains, sometimes to do battle at the water's edge, sometimes to rally in Carisbrook Castle as a last city of refuge, taught them to rely on themselves for the right to live, from the days of Richard II. to the last French descent two years before the death of Henry VIII. It was not till the reign of the Stuarts that the resident great families began to build the fine old manor houses which, like Yaverland, Knighton, and Mottstone, are now among the most ancient buildings in the island, and with the notable exception of Carisbrook Castle and some of the churches, it may be said that every town and building in the island has grown up under the protection of the forts with which Henry VIII. surrounded its coast. The economic results of the confiscation of the property of the Church by Henry VIII. are one of the puzzles of Tudor finance. The disendowment of the monasteries, when the enormous estates of the larger foundations were all thrown into the market together, must have reduced the price of land to a minimum, and given the least margin of profit to the Crown. The nobles and merchants who bought the abbey lands made good bargains, and the king, representing the State, made bad ones. Still, the sums of ready money so made must have been very large, and it is not easy to discover what became of it. The statement made by historians is that with part of the sums so raised the king endowed six new bishops' sees, and that part was spent on the fortification of the coast. The latter project sounds rather modern in conception, and no one seems to have taken particular trouble to inquire how far it was carried into effect. As a matter of fact the scheme was a patriotic and statesmanlike idea, and was executed on a scale which, considering the times, was both costly and complete. The sufferings of the Isle of Wight from the pirate forays of the French were the object-lesson which impressed the necessity for this measure on Henry VIII. and his advisers, and though the whole scheme of coast defence was applied far more elaborately to the mainland shore by the construction and armament with cannon of the castles of Deal, Walmer, Southsea, Calshot, and Hurst, and the fortification with artillery of Dartmouth and Plymouth, the good results in the case of the Isle of Wight are more easily shown. The apologists for Henry VIII. might instance the case of the ancient port of Yarmouth, at the mouth of the estuary which cuts off the "Isle of Freshwater" on the south from the centre of the island. It stands at the narrowest point of the Solent channel, opposite Hurst Castle, exposed to the attacks of any squadron approaching round the Needles.

In 1277 it was entirely burnt by the French. From that date the unfortunate little town was marked out by the French as the most convenient spot for reprisals on the English coast. It seems to have ceased to exist for a time, actually and politically. In the reign of Edward I. it sent a member to Parliament, but the privilege is said to have been suspended till the days of Elizabeth. This was not the case. It was too poor to *pay* its member's expenses. In Sir John Oglander's MS. the following note occurs: "Yarmouth is the ancientest borough town that sendeth burgesses to the Parliament for our island . . . . But it may be through poverty, as not being able to undergo the charge of sending burgesses (for all then maintained the burgesses), they lost their privileges."

The last attack made on Yarmouth by the French was in 1524, when they sacked and burnt the town, and carried off the church bells to Cherbourg, where they are said still to be kept, with the name "Yarmouth" legible on the metal. But by 1537 the king's engineers completed their new castle for the defence of Yarmouth. Church property was applied to this object in a very practical manner. Like the fortresses of Hurst and Calshot, across the water, it was built from the hewn stones of Beaulieu Abbey Church, and remains, in perfect structural repair, the most interesting of the earliest fortifications built in England for the defence of towns by artillery. It was called a "block-house," but was far larger and more formidable than the name suggests. In front was a square stone platform, mounted with eight large cannon to command the sea. This portion looks like a modern fort; but the quarters behind it for the men and officers are picturesque stone Tudor houses, with carved finials and corbels, and with remains of others of Elizabeth's time, built of brick, not unlike some of the minor offices in Hampton Court. The back of the fort is again severely practical, containing a well-built vaulted powder magazine, and the garrison kitchen, with a huge fireplace, and "lifts" to send the food up to the men's quarters above. On the east side is a finely carved Royal Arms, supported, not by the lion and unicorn, but by the lion and griffin. The whole building is an interesting mixture of feudalism, Tudorism, and modernism. Its erection marked the end of French invasions of the island. The town grew up again under cover of its guns, and by the time of James I. had so increased that he had granted it a charter and a corporation. In this charter it is stated that "Since the building of the castle the town is better inhabited than before, and that the Mayor and Burgesses, esteeming the charters before granted them insufficient to authorise them in using their liberties and immunities, had petitioned the king to make and new create them a body politic and corporate." This the king did, and Charles II. presented the corporation with a fine silver-gilt mace and seal. This, with the ancient charters, and a curious emblem in the form of a large glove fixed on a pole, which was set up for two days during a fair held on St. James's Day, to indicate that for

Yarmouth. From a drawing by R. Serle.

that time no one should on any account be committed to prison, are all that remains to attest the ancient state of the corporation. The existence of the tiny borough was denounced in Parliament, and this picturesque survival has been turned into a modern "town trust," though the old municipal insignia are still preserved.

Close by the Castle is the fine house formerly used by the Governor of the island. It is a fine example of an early Stuart mansion, panelled throughout, and with a beautiful central staircase, with the landings laid in parquet, perhaps one of the oldest examples of this kind of flooring. Lord Holmes, the conqueror of New Amsterdam, from whose captures of Guinea Gold the first guineas were coined, lived in that house, after he was made Governor of the Isle of Wight by Charles II. In the church, which, like the rest of the town, was rebuilt under the protection of the Castle, is Holmes's monument. It is said to have been part of the prize cargo of a French ship captured by him, and to have been intended as a statue of Louis XIV. of France. While it was being taken in an unfinished state to France, for the head to be modelled from the august features of the "Roi Soleil," it was taken by one of Holmes's ships. Whether this be true or not, the present head is probably a very careful, and is certainly a very spirited, portrait of the piratical Irishman, who, after serving Charles I., the French, the Germans, and the Dutch, conquered New York for England. The harsh, imperious features are chiselled with wonderful vigour and force, shaded by the Admiral's hat of the Restoration—half-cocked hat, half-plumed helmet—an interesting example of ancient naval costume.

It is said that seven churches were burnt by the French. Modern investigation reduces the number to four, one having been on the site of the Castle, and one in Fort Street. The writer was taken into a small house in this street, where a boatman and his family were having tea, and shown, in the wall of the little parlour, two low ancient pillars, *papered* over, which had formed the doorway of the old church or chapel, and were now in the party-wall of the house. Iron shot, from 4 lb. to 9 lb. weight, recently picked up at the back of the modern town, are probably relics of the French bombardment in 1524. The picturesqueness of this little town, set at the mouth of the Yar estuary, with its miniature quay, little ships, fortress, "palace," and church, is

not less than its interest as an historical object-lesson. From the west
the river is crossed by long narrow bridges and causeways, leading to the
castle and the quay. The estuary itself is not the least beautiful part
of the whole, and from its correspondence, not only in name but in
form, with the river which cuts off the down and village of Bembridge
from the centre of the island at the east corner, is a very rare and curious
instance of that occasional symmetry in physical geography which
Herodotus imagined was so far a law of nature that the course of the
Nile in Africa ought to conform to that of the Danube in Europe.
Each river has the same name, the " Yar." Each runs from south to
north, and each cuts off a high chalk down, and incloses a territory
almost exactly similar in geographical features.

The Freshwater Down on the west exactly corresponds to the
Bembridge Down on the east, the long precipice of Freshwater " Whitecliff" with Bembridge " Whitecliff," Alum Bay and its sands with
Whitecliff Bay and its sands, the beds being almost identical, though at
Bembridge the colours are less vivid, while the two peninsulas are
bounded on the north-east and north-west respectively by wide estuaries.
The reclamation of Brading Haven, and the embanking of the eastern
river Yar have somewhat altered the former lines. A map of the island,
published in 1610, shows the ancient conditions very clearly. The
eastern peninsula is there called the *Isle of Bembridge*, the western the
Isle of Freshwater ; and twelve years later it was proposed to make
the latter into a real island by cutting a trench to the sea at
Freshwater Gate, and to fortify it as a refuge and citadel in case of an
invasion.

Either of these portions might serve as an epitome of the general
scenery and character of the whole island, containing, as they do,
examples of the high downs, chalk precipices, estuaries and composite
cliffs, and lovely views of sea, land, and Solent-stream. Yet the differ-
ences are sufficient to make each of these peninsulas worth separate
study. Take, for instance, the estuaries of the eastern and western
Yar Rivers. The former has recently been reclaimed in anticipation
of the work of Nature. The estuary of the western Yar is in great
part already recovered from the sea by natural processes. The little
river which formed the valley rises within a few yards of the southern

The Solent from the Isle of Wight.

sea, at Freshwater Gate, but turning its back on the waters of the channel, flows due north towards the Solent. As its whole course is less than four miles, with a very gradual fall, it is open to the tide, and becomes a salt-water estuary within half a mile of its source. But the slob-lands on either side are rapidly being converted into firm ground. Part is covered with rough sedge-grass, which, except at high tides, is never under water. The wetter parts are thick beds of reeds, like those seen by the Norfolk Broads, between whose roots the decay of water plants is rapidly forming soil. Beyond this are squashy meadows, and outside these again rich grass lands. Looking up the estuary at sunset the scene across this mixed area of water and land is singularly rich in colour. The sunset clouds are painted again in crimson and gold on violet pools and windings of the river, and these are set and bordered with masses of yellow reeds. On either side lie the low hills, and at the head of the estuary the long aisles and tower of Freshwater Church, backed by the lofty ridge of Freshwater Down and Beacon. The gap called Freshwater Gate separates this down on the west from the Afton Down on the right. Between these lies the little bay, with the rounded shoulders of the down on either side, and the white chalk precipices rising in curve above curve, till they swing backwards towards the crowning heights of the Beacon Hill on the right, and Chale Bay on the left. Under the great down lies the home for so many years of Lord Tennyson, and between the western precipice of Scratchell's Bay and Yarmouth are the Needles, Alum Bay, and Totland Bay, making with the Freshwater Cliffs themselves perhaps the finest and most representative line of cliff scenery on the English coasts.

A visit to the seafowl colony in Freshwater Cliffs at daybreak is an island experience never forgotten. Early rising is essential for this form of morning call. On the last occasion on which the writer left Totland Bay to visit the seafowls' home the sun had not yet topped the cliffs, and the waters of the tiny bay were lying still and gray in the morning light. The crews of the small yachts moored off the bay were still asleep, the lights were not yet out in the lanterns on the masts, and were shining like dying stars. The mist was curling round the hollows above the cliffs, and still hid the sides of Freshwater Down. All the long coast line of the New Forest was hidden by a fog-bank,

and the island fortress of Hurst Castle rising above the sea opposite was
the only object visible beyond the narrow circle of the bay.

As the oars struck the water the first sunbeams streamed from over
the cliff behind, and sent a long beam of light across the Solent. The
batteries and lighthouse of Hurst flushed into rosy pink, and the
southern chalk wall of Alum Bay, the Needles, and the Needles light
were touched by the sun. The beams caught all the lines and mould-

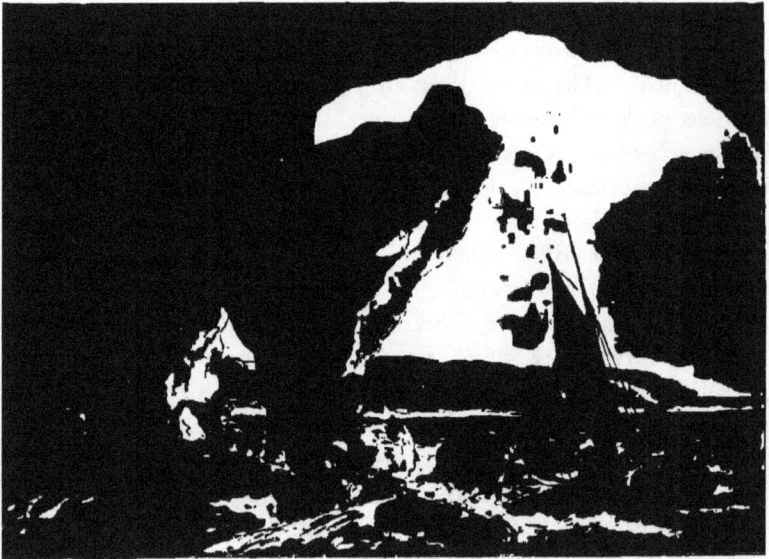

Smugglers at Freshwater Cave. From an old print.

ings of the chalk, the gray haze "dislimbed" and revealed the
structure of the rocks and precipice. At sunset the brilliant sand-
cliffs at the bottom of Alum Bay are the natural feature which
most attracts the eye. At sunrise these are in shadow, and the dominant
note is struck by the chalk precipice which forms three-quarters of
the bay, and by the jagged outline of the Needles. The rock to which
these first owed their name has disappeared. It was a sharp spine of

chalk, nearly 100 feet in height, which fell in 1764. It is probable that it was struck by lightning, just as the extreme point of the mainland cliff was recently shattered in a midnight thunderstorm and now lies in ruins on the beach. But three of the rocks remain, and the front edge of the main cliff is so similar in structure that it must in time become separated and form a fourth rock in the chain. Seen from the north the Needles and the parent cliff are like the lower jawbone of some sea monster, with the teeth awash. Nearer this resemblance increases, for the rocks do not rise squarely from their bases, but slope to a cutting edge. Between the inner rock and the cliff lies the narrow gate which leads, by one of the sudden changes only known in coast scenery, and rare even there, from the bright colours and soft outlines of Alum Bay to the grandest chalk precipice of Southern England. The Needle rocks are a kind of *propylæum* to the front of this cliff temple. As we approached the water gate between the chalk pillars, the bell of the lighthouse tolled like the morning angelus, echoing softly from rock to cliff, and on the gentle swell the boat slipped through the narrow channel and floated under the face of the highest precipice of the island. The cliff at Scratchell's Bay rises to a height of 640 feet from the water's edge, incurved, but with the section of the down itself, which is here cut across. Hence the centre of the precipice is its highest point. The whole face of the chalk is marked with regular diagonal lines of black flint. The face is hollowed for a height of nearly 200 feet from the beach, and this recess appears, when the visitor is standing below and looking seawards or skywards, as an enormous Norman arch, cut clear in the chalk against the sky. From the southern side of the bay the "Main Bench" cliff runs at an angle to the south-east. This is the main home of the sea-fowl. The chalk here has a different exposure and appears like rough concrete, "weathered" and stained in the softest tints of yellow, gray, and pink. The foot is blackened by seaweed and surge, and divided by fissures into rectangular blocks like the base of some gigantic wall.

The number of the rock-fowl, though very great, seems to have impressed most visitors to the precipices more than it did the present writer. The cliff itself is so huge that it is not in reason to suppose that its face could be "covered" with the birds, like the top of the pinnacle rock at the Farne Islands. From Sun Corner along the " Main Bench " to the Beacon at Freshwater, the chalk wall continues at a height greater than that of the cross on St. Paul's Cathedral. The top is often veiled in mist, and the impression of height, expanse, and vastness so given baffles description. It seems to reach literally from sea to sky, and the puffins, razor-bills, and guillemots on the higher ledges, or sitting in rows in the niches and crevices, look like strings of little black and white beads stretched row below row across the chalk. The noise and cries which come from the cliff are made by the gulls, the most vociferous of all sea-fowl. These are dotted all over the slopes of turf and samphire, on the lower parts of the precipice, and scream, laugh, and chatter incessantly ; while the true rock-fowl are mute until they feel some common sense of danger. Between Sun Corner and Pepper Rock is the main nesting place of the puffins and guillemots, which sit on their lofty ledges quite motionless and unconcerned until the visitor rows in close to the cliff. Then, after turning their heads towards each other like wooden puppets, a proceeding which, as seen through the glasses, produces a most comical effect as the movement passes on from line to line of the birds, some one apparently calls for " three groans for the man in the boat," and the whole concourse groan in chorus like a well-drilled political meeting. Then they fly downwards to the sea, first singly, then in flocks, and collect in little groups upon the water, though this may soon be covered with the birds without any apparent diminution in the upper ranks upon the cliff, where, safe from all danger and almost out of hearing of the waves, they sit and gaze at the intruders below.

On the water the razor-bills and puffins are so tame that they will let the boat run within a dozen yards of them. Then the whole flock disappear without sound and almost without moving the surface of the water, and presently emerge like corks at a little distance. The razor-bills swim with their beaks tilted upwards and their tails low in the water, which gives them a saucy independent air, quite unlike that of any other bird. The puffins seem all head and beak, and when they rise from the water to fly look like tin birds worked by machinery. Their wide bills, of the brightest red, blue, and yellow, hard plumage, and narrow wings are balanced by their red legs and feet, which they stick

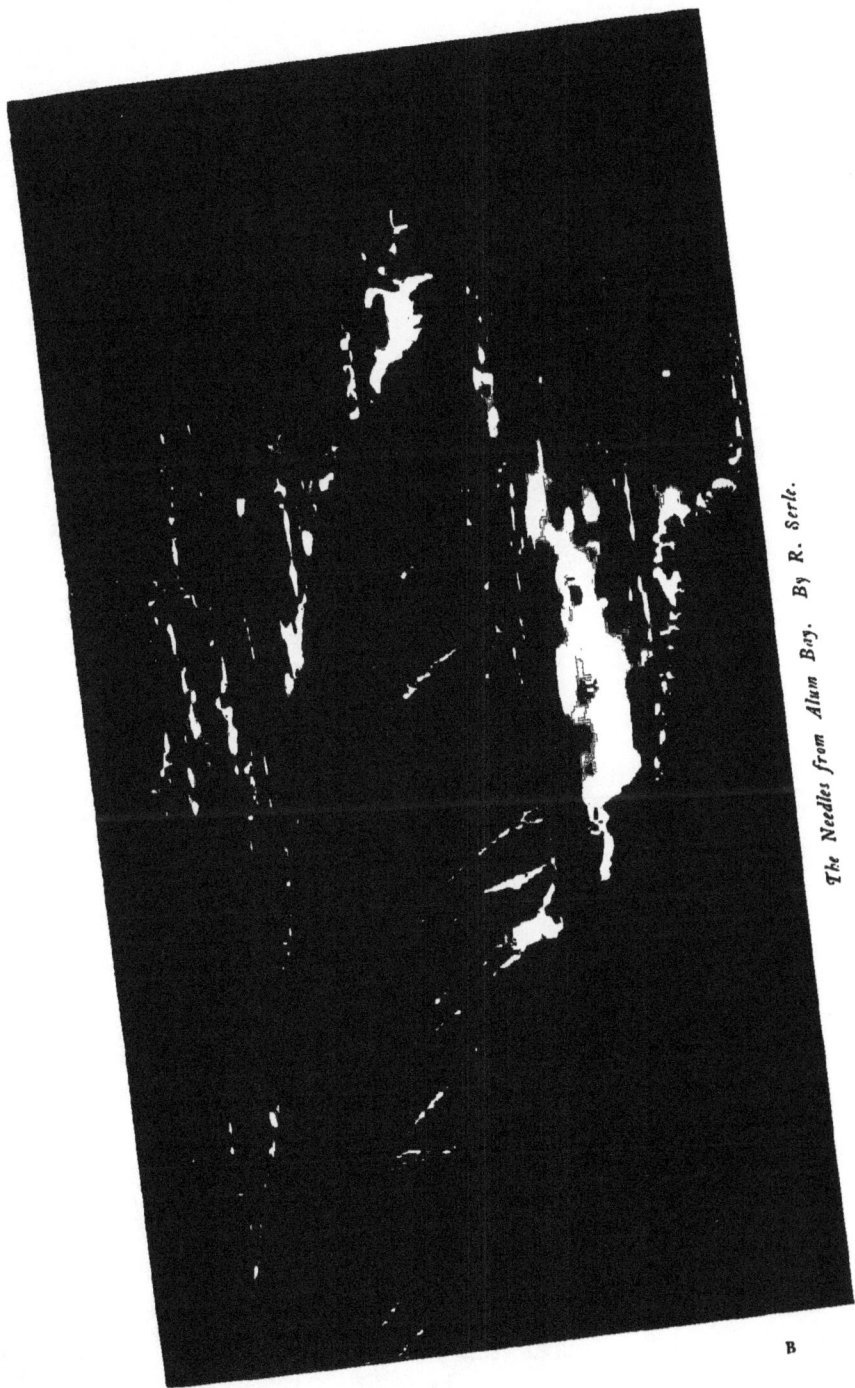

The Needles from Alum Bay. By R. Serle.

out at the widest possible angle from the line of their bodies as soon as
they leave the water.

We had scarcely finished our interview with these interesting members
of Neptune's poultry yard when a cloud of gulls flew out of the cliff,
puffins and guillemots rushed past in hundreds, and the whole colony were
thrown into sudden agitation, very different from the complacency with
which they had viewed our approach in the boat. The cause was soon

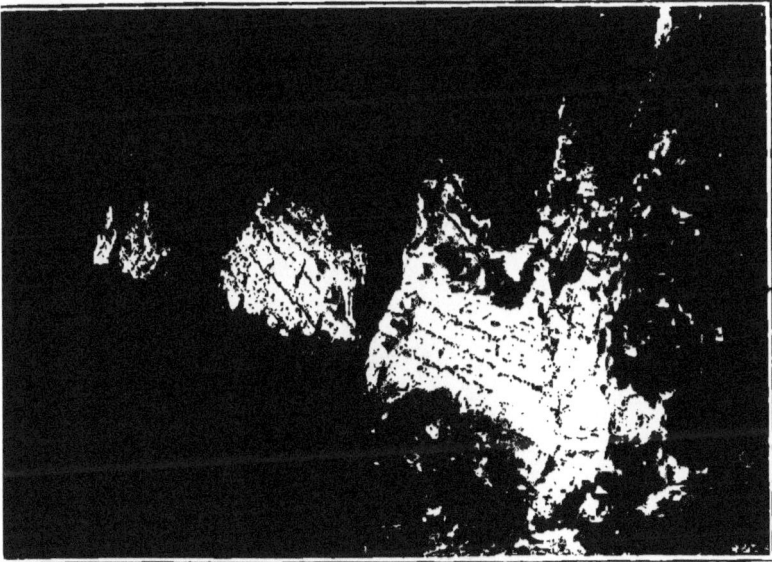

The Needles from Scratchell's Bay.   From a photograph by Messrs. F. Frith & Co.

obvious. Descending from the brow of the cliff, on a rope hardly visible
in the mist which wrapped the summit, was the figure of a man, while
two others were indistinctly seen easing the rope downward through what
appeared to be a block fastened to a post.

The climber descended some 250 feet till he came to a grass slope,
which a few minutes before had been dotted with gulls. There he slipped
his leg out of the loop in which he had been sitting, and passing the
double cord by which he had been lowered over his left arm, he walked

along the slope, stooping and picking up the gulls' eggs, which he put into a bag hanging across his chest. Above one end of the turf slope was a crack in the cliff in which a line of guillemots had been sitting. Scrambling up to this he took the eggs one by one, with as little apparent hurry as if he had been taking teacups from a shelf, and then walking back to the spot at which he had descended was hauled up to the summit, and, after removing the tackle from above, disappeared with his companions behind the brow. The adventure did not last more than ten minutes, and was evidently considered nothing unusual either by the climber or by the boatmen below.

CHAPTER II

THE CENTRAL ISLAND

Carisbrook Castle—An object-lesson in the evolution of a fortress—Successive adaptations of defence from the Celtic mound to the fortification by Genoballa, engineer of the citadel of Antwerp, to resist the Armada—Its consequent importance—Arrival and captivity of Charles I.—Sir John Oglander's account—The attempts to escape—Vigilance of Oliver Cromwell—Carisbrook village—Francheville, or Newtown—Totally destroyed by the French—Newport—Its history and burning by the French—The French general shot by Petre de Haynoe with his silver bow—Parkhurst Forest—The Medina and its likeness to the Orwell—The yachts in the Medina—Their number—Cowes—Modern yacht racing—Single-handed yachts—West Cowes Castle—Quarr Abbey—Poaching Monks—Osborne—The Queen's gardens and woods.

WHEN that distinguished French architect and antiquary, M. Viollet le Duc, wrote his *History of a Fortress,* he was probably unacquainted with Carisbrook Castle. In that delightful book, the succession of defences applied to the protection of a natural site for a fortress—very similar to that of Carisbrook—is set out with the most graphic detail, as well as great technical and historical knowledge, from the days of the primitive earth-camp, through the successive adaptations of defence to baffle the means of attack by Romans, Franks, Burgundians, and English invaders, down to the siege by the Allies in 1811, and that by the Prussians in 1870. Carisbrook Castle is probably the most perfect example in England of the evolution of a fortress, so considered. Its site marks it as the natural citadel of the island. In it every modification of the defence may be traced in historical sequence, from the primitive British camp of refuge to the mathematically perfect bastioned *enceinte* constructed after the use of artillery in sieges was fully developed, by Genoballa, the engineer of the fortress of Antwerp, who deserted from the Spaniards to take service under Queen Elizabeth, and fortified the castle against the coming invasion of the Armada. The historic growth

of the fortress is evident almost at sight, and can be verified at each step
by the known records of the island.

Stripped of every wall and tower the original Celtic earthwork would
stand as a reproduction of those which crown most of the great chalk
hills, from Winchester to Uffington Castle on the White Horse Hill.
Whit-gar, nephew of Cedric the Saxon, who built the town on the
hill opposite, stormed the old camp, and later, in due course, the whole
island was granted by the Conqueror to William Fitz-Osborne, Marshal

Carisbrook Castle.   After Luke Clennell.

of the Norman Army at the Battle of Hastings.   The Norman noble
at once built the centre and symbol of feudal ownership, the castle
keep, at the corner of the centre rampart, where it stood raised on the
top of the ancient earth-mound, just as the Round Tower of Windsor
stood alone in the days of Rufus.   Shortly after a high wall was run
round the rest of the Celtic rampart, following its outline as it stood,
and in 1086, according to the Doomsday Book, the area of the castle
grounds was twenty-six acres; for outside, and to the east of the walls

was a subsidiary Celtic camp, which was probably inclosed by barriers, though not walled. To the castle, the Conqueror summoned his half-brother, Odo of Bayeux, Archbishop of Canterbury and Earl of Kent, just as he was preparing to leave England as a candidate for the Popedom, and sentenced him to imprisonment, not as he acutely remarked, as Archbishop of Canterbury, but as the presumptuous " Earl of Kent."

No change in the defences seems to have been made until Baldwin de Redvers, who was holding the castle for the Empress Matilda, had to yield because the well in the keep ran dry. Later he dug the famous well of Carisbrook. The last of his descendants, Isabella de Fortibus, added to the buildings in the court, but not to the defences, which remained much as they were until the Wars of the Roses. Then Anthony Woodville, Lord Scales, brother of Edward IV.'s Queen, brought the fortifications up to the needs of his day, by building the great entrance gate. It is still almost perfect, and a complete example of purely military architecture as then understood. Its proportions are so picturesque and ornamental that its adaptation to its purpose is some-times forgotten. The two side-towers, pierced for hand-guns, as well as arrows, flank the whole of the straight western line of wall in addition to defending the gateway itself, the towers having been built on to the existing gate, which brings them well in front of the old wall. Between the towers, and over the gate, is a machicolated gallery, from the open base of which missiles or boiling water could be discharged vertically upon the heads of the stormers. A portcullis, and strong double doors, the latter still standing, completed this carefully thought-out defence. Henry VIII., fearing for the island in his French wars, then made the first modification for the use of cannon. At the south, east, and north-east corners, the old wall was cleverly extended into small bastions, called " knights," in each of which cannon were mounted, and the castle was to that extent modernised. The list of defensive implements kept in the castle at this time is preserved, and is a curious relic of the transition period in the art of war. The armament of the castle was " 5 pieces of iron ordnance, 520 shot, 23 double barrels and 3 firkins of powder ; 140 hackbuts ; 59 chests of arrows ; 3 barrels of bowstrings ; 500 morris pikes, javelins, and bills." But the final adaptation of the fortress to the new way of war was made by order of Queen Elizabeth. The castle, with its keep, walls, and "knights," was kept as a central citadel, but surrounded by a complete parallelogram of bastioned defences, still in perfect preservation, and adapted to the site with the skill of a master hand, trained in the wars of the Low Countries and Italy—the highest school of the military art. Genoballa inclosed the whole hill-top, outside the Celtic ramparts, by a regular pentagonal wall, having a bastion at each corner mounted with cannon, outworks in the moat to cover the curtains, and solid stone ramparts. The lower part of the Celtic works he cleverly adapted as a second line of defence on the east side, paring them into the shape of bastions, and forming what is called a "hornwork," with guns mounted at the corners. The whole design is very little inferior to the later system perfected by Vauban, and is a unique instance in this country of such a fortification.

It was this almost impregnable fortress of which Colonel Robert Hammond had charge, when Charles I. arrived as an unbidden guest. Its importance to the Parliament may be better understood from the foregoing description than it was by ordinary Englishmen even at that day, when Andrew Marvel himself clearly understood it to be a mere feudal castle when he speaks of "Carisbrooke's narrow case." If Colonel Hammond and the islanders had joined him, Charles might have held Carisbrook with some hopes of success, while he played off the Parliament against the army. Hence the extreme anxiety shown in Cromwell's letters to "Dear Robin," as he calls Colonel Hammond, the Governor of Carisbrook. But Hammond was staunch and prudent, and the town of Newport was so wholly for the Parliament as to neutralise the personal loyalty to the king of the leading families in the island.

Sir John Oglander, of Nunwell, whose family had held that estate in lineal descent, as he remarks in his quaint diary, since the days of Henry I., has left, among the interesting personal experiences with which his notes are filled, an account of the reception of the king in the island. Charles was evidently very much broken in spirit. His last visit to the island had been paid to review his troops before the expedition to Rochelle and the assassination of the Duke of Buckingham. He now appeared almost as a suppliant. "Sondaye morninge," writes Sir John Oglander, "att churche I heard a rumour that ye King wase that nyght, beinge ye

Entrance to Carisbrook Castle. From an engraving by T. Stevens, 1785.

14th of November, landed at Cows. I confesse I coold not beleeve itt, but att evening prayor ye same daye Sir Robert Dyllington sent his servant to mee to inform mee of his Maties coming into ye island, and that our governor, Col. Hammon, commanded mee and my sonn (as he had done all ye gentlemen of ye island) to meet him att Nuport ye nexte daye, being Mondaye, by nine in ye mornynge. Truly this news trobled mee very mutch : but on Mondaye mornynge I went to Nuport, where I found most of ye gentlemen of ye islande ; and not longe after Hammon came and he made a short speache to us, which as well as my olde memorie will give me leafe, wase thus, or to this purpose— Gentlemen, I beleeve it was as straunge to you as to mee to hear of his Maties comynge into this island. Hee informs mee necessitie broughte him hithor, and theyre weare a sorte of people neare Hampton Coorte (from whence he came) that had voted and were resolved to murder him (or woordes to that effect) ; and therefore soe privately he was forced to come awaye, and soe to thrust himself upon this island, hoping to bee here secure."

Colonel Hammond then stated his determination to secure the king's person, and the measures he had taken to guard the entrances to the island until he had an answer to an express which he had sent to Parliament. Sir Robert Dyllington on behalf of the gentlemen of the island then requested permission for them to visit the king, and "express their dewties to him," to which Hammond consented, remarking "truely I woold invite you all to dinner, had I anie entertaynments ; but truely I want extremely fowle for his Matie ; intimatinge thereby that he wanted ye gentlemen theyre assistance."

The king seems to have heard of this piece of vicarious begging on Hammond's part, for after receiving Sir John and the rest, and repeating his reasons for leaving Hampton Court, he added, " I desior not a drop moore of Christian bloude showlde bee spilt, neythor do I desior to bee chargeable to anye of you ; I shall not desior soe much as a capon from anye of you, my resolution in coming here being to bee secure till some happy accomodacion bee mayde."

Colonel Hammond's statement to the gentlemen of the island as to his ignorance of the king's intentions is irreconcilable with the accounts describing Colonel Hammond's visit to Charles at Titchfield near Southampton, at which he had given a guarded promise to receive and protect him in the island.

The king remained in the island from November 23rd, 1647, until November 29, 1648, when he was seized by the soldiers, exasperated by the outbreak of the "second civil war," and carried off to the lonely fortress of Hurst, and thence to London to be tried at Westminster.

With the exception of an interval after September 18th, 1648, in which he was allowed to reside at the Grammar School at Newport, during negotiations with the Parliament in the absence of the army, which was fighting in the north, the king was all this time a prisoner at Carisbrook, his confinement varying in rigour according as Parliament or the army had the control of affairs. The personal history of his confinement is given at immense length in the papers and writings of the time. Cromwell seems to have been supplied with information not accessible even to Hammond, constantly keeping the governor informed of attempts which had been, or were to be, made at rescue—just as Napoleon, at Paris, was able to warn his marshals in Spain of intrigues and plots which were going on in their own provinces. Hammond's first information of the attempt made by the king to escape from the castle on March 20th, 1648, was in a letter from Cromwell, written on April 6th. The king was then living in the centre of the castle court, in the building which is now the governor's house. Mr. Firebrace, the king's confidential attendant, had arranged with Mr. John Newland of Newport, Mr. Edward Worsley of Gatcombe, and Mr. Osborne, usher to the king, to have horses ready to take the king to the seaside, where he was to embark in a large boat. The king was to lower himself from the window and be met by Firebrace, who would see him across the court, over the wall at the back of the castle, and across the bowling green. Charles was physically utterly unfitted for enterprises of this kind. He made no experiments until the night for action came, and then found that he could not pass between the bars, a difficulty which Firebrace had foreseen and begged him to provide against by cutting a bar. Cromwell not only gave a correct account of this attempt, but foretold the method of the next in the following letter to Colonel Hammond :—

"Intelligence came to the hands of a very considerable person that the king attempted to get out of his window and that he had a cord of silk with him whereby to slip down, but his breast was so big, the bar would not give him passage. This was done in one of the dark nights about a fortnight ago. . . . The guard that night had some quantity of wine with them. The same party assures us that there is *aqua fortis* gone down from London to remove that obstacle which hindered, and that the same design is to be put in execution the next dark night." Again in another

King Charles I.'s Window, Carisbrook Castle. By R. Serle.

letter, dated April 22nd, he writes, " The *aqua fortis* was spilt by the way by accident, but yesterday about four o'clock, a fat plain man carried to the king a hacker, which is an instrument made here on purpose to make the king's two knives, which he hath by him, cut as saws. The time assigned is May Day at night for the king's escape, but it may be sooner if opportunity serves."

Colonel Hammond acted on this information, so far as to remove the king to another set of rooms, built against the main wall of the castle, with windows looking over the old-scarp and moat, towards Carisbrook village. They were on the right of the main gate, and still remain, one being open, and the other, and smaller window, that from which the king was to make his second attempt, being blocked with masonry. The larger window, which was that of the king's sitting-room, was fitted with new bars, and a sentry was set below that of the bedroom. There, too, the bars were close, and the king, instructed by his perilous failure, cut one through with a saw, which he had made from a knife-blade, by means of the "hacker" referred to in Cromwell's letter. But the plot had been betrayed, and not only were the sentries below increased, but one Major Rolfe, a fanatical officer, was waiting armed with pistols to shoot him dead if he descended. Colonel Hammond had also placed an ambuscade to intercept Mr. Worsley and Mr. Osborne, who galloped past them and received their fire unhurt, owing to the darkness.

The country round the castle is probably little changed in appearance since the early days of Charles's captivity, when he was treated as a guest rather than as a prisoner, and allowed to visit Sir John Oglander and hunt in Parkhurst Forest. The pretty village of Carisbrook, with its fine church tower, stands on the hill opposite the castle, just as the church and town of Conisborough in Yorkshire cover a twin mound to that on which is the very similar castle of Conisborough, so well known to the readers of *Ivanhoe*. A bright trout stream, with its mill pond and water-wheel separates the two hills, and runs down to Newport to join the Medina. To follow this stream down from the ancient fortress to the modern capital of the island, and thence by the principal river to the principal port at Cowes is an expedition full of interest. By the Carisbrook stream above Newport, with its mill pools and ancient mills, is the pleasantest approach to the town ; and the contrast of the tidal river into which the brook falls at a short distance below its springs is one of the many abrupt surprises in scenery which the island furnishes. The Medina creek runs right up between the houses, and the masts of the lighters and small coasters rise among the roofs of this inland town.

Newport is not the ancient capital of the island. Its rise, like the decay of Yarmouth, was caused by the French invasions. The original capital of the island was at Newtown, anciently called Francheville, which stands, or rather stood, on an estuary between Yarmouth and Cowes. This was the natural port of the island in the days of the early Angevin kings, facing their harbour at Lymington, whither they came from their capital at Winchester, through the royal domain of the New Forest. Arrived at Newtown, the king found the best natural harbour in the island, with a depth of water sufficient to float a 500-ton ship, on the borders of another royal forest, that of Avington or Parkhurst, which stretched from

Newport. By John Fullwood.

the harbour of Newtown to the gates of Carisbrook. It is not flattering to English pride to know that this natural capital had to be deserted owing to foreign invasion. In the reign of Richard II. in 1377, the French burnt it to the ground, and though it was rebuilt, and called *Newtown*, it never recovered its prosperity ; nothing remains to show its former dignity except an ancient wooden town hall, and lanes and fields, which still retain the names of the streets and buildings which once stood upon them—High Street, Gold Street, Quay Street, and Draper's Alley.

There is no other instance in England of so complete a destruction of a
town by foreign conquest. It remained a " rotten borough " after it
ceased to exist as a town, and was represented by John Churchill—afterwards the Duke of Marlborough, and by Mr. Canning ! Newport,
though so near to Carisbrook, was also burnt by the French in the same
invasion, and was for two years left utterly deserted. The French
Armada seems to have landed at St. Helen's Point, almost opposite
Southsea, at the eastern end of the island, and sacked and burnt every
considerable place from thence to Yarmouth, with the exception of Carisbrook Castle itself. This was besieged, but the French general was shot,
and the siege raised, as recorded by Sir John Oglander in the following
quaint note, one of a series written on the ancient families of the
island.

"The de Haynoes were Lords of Stenbury, when ye Ffrench had
taken ye island, and beseyghed Caresbroke Castle. One Petrus de
Haynoe came to Sir Hugh Tyrell, then Captayne of ye Island, and told
him he woold undertake with his sillver bowe to kill ye Commander
of ye ffrench, taking his tyme, for he had observed how nyghtes and
morninges he came near ye Castle ; which on leave he killed out of a
loopehold on ye west syde of ye Castle, and by that meanes brought ye
ffrench to take a composition of 2,000 markes to begone, and to doe no
further harme ; on which embassage one of ye Oglanders wass imployed
and effected it." The French also exacted a promise that if they chose
to return in a year's time the inhabitants were not to offer any resistance to their landing. But the French were also defeated, according
to tradition, in an ambuscade set by Sir Hugh Tyrrel near the castle,
at a place now called " Deadman's Lane." Newport was again burnt by
the French in the reign of Edward IV. ; but the houses are sufficiently
good and old to make it a pretty old county town ; there are many
quaint cupolas and weather-vanes ; good old brick houses with pro-
jecting upper windows ; and in St. Thomas's Square one very fine
house, now divided into shops, with deep cornices below the roof,
carved window jambs, and a porch modelled like a shell over the door,
like the ancient Fairfax house, now pulled down, at Putney, and with an
appearance of antiquity far beyond anything else in the town.

Parkhurst Forest, which reaches from near Newport to the Newtown estuary, is a very good example of what a national forest ought *not* to be, and of what the New Forest would have become had the old Act empowering its inclosure as a State timber farm not been modified. It is an ancient royal forest ; but instead of remaining in its natural condition of a wild furze heath and woodland it is now a solid mass of timber, mainly oak and chestnut, viewless, and almost impenetrable except by the roads cut through it. If any one desires to know how dull a thousand acres of scientific plantation can be he need only spend an

Cowes. By John Fullwood.

hour in Parkhurst Forest. On the other hand it is an economic success. The whole of the land running from Parkhurst to Yarmouth is obviously poor, sour clay and gravel, bad for crops of any kind, and rapidly going out of cultivation, or cultivated in the poorest way. If it had all been planted fifty years ago it would now cost little and pay well. Now the land is a failure from every point of view, financial or picturesque. The tidal Medina river, which cuts the island in half in a straight line from Newport to Cowes, is singularly like the Suffolk Orwell,

c

Newport taking the place of Ipswich and Cowes of Harwich, the point of difference being that the land on either side is hilly down to the coast instead of gradually coming down to sea level.

The tide soon runs out and leaves the river bed a level lake of mud, from which cement is made in the only "factory" in the island. But the brigs and ketches lying among the fields, the old brick tide mill, many stories high, in which French prisoners used to be kept in the old war, and the fine timber which runs down from Whippingham church make the upper reaches picturesque enough. Lower the Medina is one vast storage for yachts. Their numbers are quite incredible ; they lie in hundreds packed close together, from the 500-ton three-masted steam yacht to the half-rater for racing single-handed. Yachts never "die." They are scarcely ever lost at sea, or sold to be broken up, or burnt, or blown up. They are so well built that without such accidents they do not decay, and fashion, which has during the past twelve or fifteen years turned yachts into racing machines, in which owing to the constant improvements in rig and design the last constructed usually wins, has multiplied their number out of all proportion to the demand for them as mere private ships for living in and cruising. The depreciation in capital value of these hundreds of yachts laid up in the Medina, would, if ascertained, be some measure of the margin of income available for the gratification of the luxury of yacht-racing in this country.

Lately a more sensible view has prevailed, and small yacht racing, in which the owner sails his own boat and enjoys a contest of seamanship rather than of mechanical design has become the favourite amusement of the Solent. Lord Pembroke has given a brightly written account of this in the "Badminton" series. But yacht-racing on the large scale has made Cowes what it is, the brightest and daintiest of English ports. The pretty harbour full of yachts in commission, the ancient Tudor fort of West Cowes Castle—now the club house of the Royal Yacht squadron—and the modern East Cowes Castle on the opposite hill, make a beautiful approach to the old town. It is a port without commerce, dirt, or noise, whose only trade is that of providing the details, fittings, and equipment of the most luxurious playthings of the richest people in the world. Nothing on earth is quite so gloriously bright, smart, clean, and tidy as an English man-of-war. The harbour, town, and yachts of Cowes are apparently all voluntarily devoted to the reproduction of this ideal as an end in itself.

The representation in miniature of the social and political life of mediæval England in the Isle of Wight, would not have been complete

West Cowes Castle. After Peter De Wint, 1818.

without the addition of one of the great religious foundations. This was supplied by the foundation of Quarr Abbey, by Baldwin de Redvers, Earl of Devon, Lord of the island, in the reign of Henry I. It was to the Cistercian order that the earl looked to serve the abbey which he founded, and in later reigns this great foundation rivalled the splendour

c 2

of Netley and Beaulieu Abbeys, the two great Cistercian houses which stood on the two estuaries of "Hampton" and Beaulieu on the opposite side of the Solent. The Abbots of Quarr became almost petty princes, and were frequently associated with the captains of the island in securing its defence from invasion. In 1340 the abbot was nominated sole warden by Edward III., and converted the abbey into a fortress. The whole precinct was surrounded by a strong wall, like that which incloses the ruins of Beaulieu, large enough to give a refuge to all the inhabitants of that part of the island. Access to the sea was by a fortified gate with portcullis defences, and a beacon tower was built to signal across the Solent the approach of danger. This sea-gate of the abbey, Ryde—then called "La Rye," and Cowes, were the only points from which boats were allowed to leave the island for the mainland. The French burnt Ryde, but the garrison of the Abbey seems to have been able to defend itself successfully. The Cistercians of Quarr were bound by the rules of their order to abstain from flesh ; but like Chaucer's monk, they seem to have taken liberal views of their vows in the later days of the establishment, and

> " Recked not of that text a pulled hen,
> That saith that hunters been not holy men."

They poached the Manor of Ashey, and the record of their transgressions is kept in the rolls of the manor. It would be interesting to know how these " presentments " were viewed by the abbey authorities. Did they condone the clerical offence in consideration of the improvement in fare at the refectory table? Or were the poachers corrected by penance, vigils, and bread and water? In the rolls of another manor, we find that one Hardekyn, a clerk, was incorrigible. Rabbits were his temptation. He shot them over the warren fence with a bow and arrow. Thrice he was seen to do so—"iii. *cuniculos sagittis transfixit*." " Three rabbits with arrows he transfixed." How did he account to the sacristan for their appearance at the common table?

" Ha, Brother Hardekyn, rabbit pie again? How is this?"

" *Domestici*—domestic or tame rabbits, if it please you, Master Sacristan. I have a dispensation, and am permitted to keep rabbits in my cell, and their increase is singularly blessed."

Infatuated Hardekyn ! He would not be warned ; he was taken

red-handed ; put *in vincula.* Chains and prison were his lot till he threw himself in *misericordiam dominæ,* on the mercy of the Lady of the Manor.

The abbey has now almost as completely vanished as the records of its inhabitants. Parts of the wall of the precinct, a fragment of the abbot's kitchen, and of the guest house alone remain, converted into a house and farm buildings. The abbey church and all its subsidiary

Quarr Abbey. By John Fullwood.

buildings were pulled down by John Mills, a Southampton merchant, who bought it after its confiscation, and the material sold as building stone.

Those who are interested in the change of ideas in the matter of sites for houses will find matter for reflection in the contrast between the positions chosen by the builders of Quarr Abbey and Osborne respectively.

The builders of each were probably ahead of their time in their views as to what constituted a desirable site for an establishment of the first order, both in size and from the social rank of its owners. But the builders of the abbey, like the builders of Osborne, had no thought, when first selecting their site, of choosing one suited for defence. Like other ecclesiastics, they enjoyed the rare privilege of making their house for convenience, not for safety, and they chose to place it in a valley sloping gently to the sea, sheltered on either side by low wooded hills, at the back by a higher ridge, watered by a brook, and having on one side an ever-lasting spring. Warmth, wood, water, and ready access to the Solent sea made this an ideal site, according to mediæval notions. Osborne, like Quarr Abbey, stands on an estate facing the Solent, and on that estate a similar site was available. But the house, or palace, for its design and dimensions are on the largest scale, is not placed in the shelter near the sea. It stands on the uplands at the head of the seaward valley. Space, air, and a wide view are advantages more in keeping with modern requirements than the quiet and warmth of the valley. The ruins of Quarr are seen as a surprise, just as Beaulieu Abbey is invisible until the edge of the valley is reached. The towers of Osborne are a landmark. Driving over the high land of Palmer's Hill, between Quarr Abbey and Cowes, the scene is almost a reproduction of that on the high land above the Orwell near Ipswich. The Medina takes the place of the Orwell, and a minor feature of resemblance is the careful farming of the Queen's estate of 8,000 acres, the large fields, the clipped thorn hedges, and the new plantations. Osborne is a fine instance of how a site can be *made* beautiful. Its height and the view of the Solent were the only features contributed by Nature. Human skill and taste have done the rest. The great Italian villa, with its yellow walls, terraces and towers, is surrounded at the back by timber exactly suited to its character—clumps of ilexes, groves of cork-trees, single cedars, deodars, and spreading Mediterranean pines. Among these are the indigenous hard-wood trees. But the principal idea has been to produce surroundings different to those of the common English mansion, and to make the most of the unusual and south European landscape.

The taste and care of the late Prince Consort are amply justified by the results. There is nothing in the south of England quite like the seaward view from Osborne terrace. The formal garden melts into wide lawns dropping, between the rounded sides of the valley. These are studded with clumps of arbutus, masses of rhododendrons, or pines, at a sufficient distance to break the lines without diminishing the sense of space. At the valley end the blue Solent fills the picture, framed on either side by sloping lines of wood.

CHAPTER III

"THESE mountains," remarked a matter-of-fact tourist in the Italian lakes, "appear to have no *feet;*" by which was meant that the slope rises straight from the water, with none of the usual fringe of beach and *débris.* The Boniface down at Ventnor makes a nearer approach to this peculiarity of the Italian and Mediterranean mountains than any part of the English coast. The smooth grassy chalk down slopes at an angle almost too steep to climb, from a height of 800 feet almost to the edge of the sea. The top is so straight and level, the slope so regular and uniform, that it looks like an enormous earthwork rising from the sea. But before reaching the sea level the sloping chalk ceases, and gives place to a perpendicular face of broken stone, like the masonry scarp at the bottom of an earthen rampart. This continues for many miles, rising gradually to the west in the direction of St. Catharine's Point and Black Gang Chine, till it becomes a high rugged wall of sandstone, like one of the "scarrs" which jut out at the top of a Yorkshire moorside. From its summit the sloping hills and downs still rise. Hence its name, the *Undercliff.* Over it the earth constantly slides and topples in masses great and small, and by slow degrees has formed a shelf, now broad, now narrow, between the Undercliff and the sea. On the shelves, and against the face of this cliff below St. Boniface Down, the Ventnor people have built their houses, like the puffins and guillemots in the

Freshwater precipices, sheltered from all rough winds by the monster down above them. The "discovery" of Ventnor and the Undercliff only dates from the last fifty years, when Sir James Clark wrote, " It is a matter of surprise to me, after having fully examined that favoured spot, that the advantages which it possesses in so eminent a degree in point of shelter and position should have been so long overlooked in

Drawn by P. Dewint. *W. B. Cooke fecit.*

Shore near Ventnor. After Peter De Wint.

a country like this, whose inhabitants have been traversing half the globe in search of a climate."

The search for a climate made Ventnor ; but the beauty of the Undercliff is enough to satisfy the most robust traveller. This narrow irregular shelf, backed by the wall of cliff, has a double share of spring and catches the last breath of summer. Little rich meadows nestle under the crags between cliff and sea, woods and groves of ash, sycamore, beech, and maple cluster on the slopes, showing that form of beauty scarcely seen elsewhere in England, trees and foliage

outlined against a background of blue sea. This juxtaposition of trees
and fertility, with cliff and sea, lasts for several miles west of Ventnor.
Beyond Steephill Castle are narrow meadows at the foot of the crags ;
broken rocks crop out from turf which is rich with primroses and
flowers ; the cliff is hung with ivy and moss, maples and rowans grow
from the crevices, as on a Scotch hillside, and in places the turf is studded
with ancient thorns smothered with wild clematis. Above all this the
rock pigeons and jackdaws swing out from the upper ledge of the cliff,
and below is heard the suck and surge of the Channel sea. At St.
Lawrence the timber is even finer. Springs break out from the cliff foot,
and give the sight and sound of running water. Beyond the spring
are Pelham woods, tall trees, mainly sycamores, full of nesting rooks, one
of the few instances of a rookery by the sea.

The change from all this warmth and prettiness of the Undercliff to
what Dr. Johnson would have described as " deformity and horror " is
very sudden. The line of the cliffs trends more to the north-west beyond
the village of Niton ; the trees dwindle and disappear, the cliff wall
above, now bare, corrugated, and weather-worn, mounts higher and
higher, and on the left the evidences of recent landslips and disturbance
of the surface increase. It is like the change from the vineyards of Etna
to the region of invading lava, though water, not fire, has here been the
destroying agent. At St. Catharine's Point all the prettiness has gone.
Here at the most southern point of the island, where it juts furthest into
the Channel waves, and where every ship passing up or down the sea-road
by day sends news of its safety to London, the scenery is far more wild
and forbidding than any presented by the giant chalk precipices east and
west of the island. The profile of the point seen towards the west
descends in "knees," from the down 600 feet above, to the point on
which the most powerful lighthouse in the world warns ships from
approaching the sunken rocks which extend from this broken and
unquiet land beneath the surface of the sea. The " knees " are the cliff
faces from which the land has slipped. Below each is an irregular slope
of earth and rocks in such disorder and confusion as to produce a sense
not only of irregularity but of ugliness. In places the "slip" is going
on still. Here the ground looks as if a thousand navvies had been
excavating a reservoir, or piling some huge embankment ; rivers of half-

soaked mud, clay, and loam, turf detached and sliding on the surface, stones half embedded, and curiously coloured earths, poured down the hollows of the cliffs and slopes, are the evidences that the alterations in the level of land may be rapid and unexpected, without the need for any great " convulsion of nature," even in our time. The springs and rain

The Undercliff, near Ventnor. By John Fullwood.

wash out a layer of bluish clay which lies beneath the sandstone crag. The crag then topples down and rolls to the foot of the clay slope. Then the exposed clay slides down over the fallen rocks and in time undermines a second shelf of cliff. Below St. Catharine's Down these slips form rivers of clay and rocks extending many hundred feet. Two enormous fragments stand on either side of the road, which is itself protected by strong low walls against the rolling rocks, which might at any time fall and block it. One of the largest landslips in this part of the Undercliff took place in 1799, and was described by the rector of Niton, who saw it. "The whole of the ground from the cliff above," he wrote, "was seen in motion, which motion was directed towards the sea, nearly in a straight line. The ground above, beginning with a great founder from the base of the cliff, kept gliding down, and at last rushed on with violence totally changing the surface of all the ground to the west of the brook that runs into the sea, so that now the whole is con-vulsed and scattered about as if done by an earthquake. Everywhere are chasms that a horse or cow might sink into and disappear." Between St. Catharine's Point and Black Gang Chine is yet another form of coast scenery. The road runs under a line of stratified *yellow* sandstone cliff rising from a setting of close turf. The ground sloping from the road to the sea is of the "tumultuous" kind, much given to slipping and disorder. But the long line of sandstone cliff above is singularly beautiful. It is seamed by innumerable deep horizontal shelves eaten out by the weather, and these again are divided vertically by rounded hollows, so that the whole surface of the cliff is marked by tier above tier of ornamental mouldings. The colour is a rich warm yellow; but on the ledges and shelves of the rock so many gray, orange, and purple lichens, and patches of sea-pink grow, that the colour of the whole is a blend of yellow, gray, and pink. Above Black Gang Chine this cliff ends in a great bastion, the home of hundreds of jackdaws and stock-doves and many kestrels. So few persons ever leave the shore or road to pry into the upper cliff that the birds are quite tame; and at midday when the hot sun warms the shelves of rock the whole cliff face is musical with the cooing of the stock-doves, while others with the jackdaws drop in from over the summit from moment to moment, and spreading their wings descend like parachutes to their resting places on the crag.

The Black Gang Chine is as desolate and unattractive as the yellow cliffs above it are bright and beautiful. "Chine" is in Dorsetshire and Hampshire, the name given to any part of a cliff which is so broken as to allow an ascent from the beach to the ground above. Along the Bournemouth shore these "chines" are often singularly beautiful, their sides covered with heather, fern, and flowers, and rhododendrons, while

Blackgang Chine. After Peter De Wint.

often a clear stream runs through the bottom. The name extends to the Isle of Wight, and Luccombe Chine, east of Ventnor, need not fear comparison with the most beautiful of those on the mainland coast of Hampshire. But Black Gang Chine, which descends for more than 200 feet from the verge to the sea, is a natural channel for the gradual ooze and subsidence of black clay, iron gray marl, and *débris*, which the streamlet and land springs are constantly diluting till they are set in motion, and crawl in sluggish streams, like cooling lava, to the sea. Its

Brighstone Church. By R. Serle.

appearance is more strange than beautiful, but from the eastern verge of the funnel the whole of the " Back of the Island " is seen as far as the Needle Rocks, a wide bight, with a coast-line of twenty miles without a single harbour or break, by any considerable river or estuary in the long forbidding line of cliffs. No town, or anything larger than a fishing hamlet breaks this desolate coast. Here begins the wide, flat, cultivated plain which runs back through the centre of the island to Newport. It is as purely agricultural a district as any in High Suffolk or Cambridgeshire, unwatered by rivers, harbourless where it touches the coast, and reminded that it is bounded by the sea only when some more than unusually notable shipwreck, such as that of the *Eider*, takes place on the Atherfield Rocks. This plain is bounded on the west by the line of chalk downs which hits the coast between Brook and Freshwater, and runs on in that tremendous line of chalk precipices, broken only by the cove of Freshwater Gate, till it is cut short across as if by a knife at Scratchell's Bay. Beneath their inland front lies Brighstone, or Brixton, the parish of which Bishop Ken and Samuel Wilberforce were rectors, and where William Wilberforce the elder, died.

East of Ventnor, towards Dunnose Point, there is no such sudden change from beauty to desolation as takes place beyond St. Catharine's Point. The woods and streams of Bonchurch which lie beneath the buttressed wall of the down, widen out into a broad and beautiful wilderness known as the Landslip. Its appearance belies its rather ominous name. It has nothing in common with the squalor and confusion of the landslips west of Ventnor. Probably the fall of cliff was on such an immense scale, that all movement has since ceased, and nature has had time to repair and beautify the ruins, aided by the finest climate in England. Some two hundred acres of ground, studded with groves, thickets, and rocks, and covered with innumerable flowers, are backed by a semicircular wall of cliff on the north, and washed below by the Channel waves. The cliff is as beautifully wooded as the ground at its foot. It resembles the coombes and gorges in the Mendip Hills ; ivy, moss, and yellow wallflowers, spring out of every crevice, and trees and shrubs, rise level with the fields which run up to the crest of the ravine. Thence the eye looks level with their tops, or searches the whole of the glades and recesses of the sea-girt wood hundreds of feet below. From the hill above the Landslip, across the wide waters of Sandown Bay, are seen the long white wall of Culver Cliffs, and the fortress on the summit of Bembridge Down.

. The Landslip may be said to mark the eastern, as St. Catharine's Point does the western end of the Undercliff region. It is by far the most obviously pretty, unusual, and attractive portion of the island, from what must be called the " modern " point of view. Fifty years ago it was unknown to the world, and scarcely visited even by the islanders. This was less strange than might be supposed. The huge

Ibsenkirche

Luccombe Chine. By John Fullwood.

down shut it off from the rest of the island like a wall. Even now, when the train emerges from the tunnel through Boniface Down there is an impression analogous to that which might be produced by a journey through the centre of a Maritime Alp, and an arrival on the shore of the Mediterranean. Except for the tiny meadows, the Undercliff was not cultivated, and could not be cultivated, hence there was no temptation to migrate there.

The inland slope was long a favourite district ; on it is one of the finest houses in the island, Appledurcomb, the home of the Worsley family, so often referred to by Sir John Oglander. But beyond its crest the ancient population of the island did not care to penetrate.

CHAPTER IV

BRADING AND THE "ISLE OF BEMBRIDGE"

ANY inquirer into the history of the Isle of Wight, however limited his researches, will look back with pleasure to the day on which he first made acquaintance with the personality of Sir John Oglander of Nunwell, whose ancient house still stands near Brading.

He is a link between the old and the new, between Isabella de Fortibus, the last of the feudal lords—in this case a lady—of the island, who is a very real and living person in Sir John's mind, when in historical vein, and the mixed and conflicting modern era of county councils and centralisation. The head of an ancient and distinguished family, who had held their estate in the island since the days of Henry I.—they hold it still—he was in the reign of James I. and Charles I. *the representative man*, of what he fondly calls "owre island." It would take more space than is available, and is perhaps scarcely necessary in this short notice of the island, to dwell on the evidences of unusual culture and education which the leading country gentlemen of this period possessed. It is evident from most of the voluminous writings of the Revolution that in addition to native wit, there was much education and refinement as well as practical experience and good sense among the landed proprietors on both sides, in the struggles of the Revolution. Sir John himself was educated at Balliol, as was his father before him. But he makes no claims on this account, though his admiration for his friend Sir Richard Worsley of Appledurcomb, whose descendant, a later Sir Richard Worsley, made such good use of Sir John's artless writings in his valuable *History of the Isle of Wight*, constantly betrays his respect for "ye mann of learning." But Sir John was observant, genial, and quaintly in earnest. Circumstances placed him among the leading men of his country—for the Wight was even then more detached in interests from the "adjacent island of Great Britain" than is readily conceivable at this short distance of time ; and he was impelled to set down from day to day, in his own quaint phrase, an account of events and persons, ranging from his reception of Charles I., whether in the days of his prosperity, when he visited the island as a mighty monarch to review his troops destined for the French war, or later in his lowest fortunes as a refugee, to the merits or failings of his country neighbours, and the pattern of the new French clogs which he brought as a present to his lady. Much of the "Oglander manuscript" has been published.[1] Much still remains unprinted at Nunwell his ancient home. But whatever the subject of Sir John's remarks he is always shrewd and original. His accounts of contemporary matter are freely referred to in other chapters. Here we propose to present the reader to the Knight of Nunwell himself, as he wrote down what he saw and thought in "owre island " from day to day.

Sir John on himself.

[This extract is purely personal, and the quaint element predominates. Sir John had written an obituary notice of his father, Sir William Oglander, and pleased with the effect, went on to do the same for himself. He became "rather mixed " at times, between the third and first person, being unused to the form of composition known as " writing one's own epitaph."]

---

[1] *Extracts from the MSS. of Sir John Oglander, Kt., of Nunwell, deputy-governor of Portsmouth, deputy-lieutenant of the Isle of Wight.* Edited, with an introduction and notes, by W. H. Long. Portsmouth : W. H. Long, 120 High Street.

"The life of Sir John Oglander, Knight, who came to keepe house at Nunwell, Anno Dom. 1607, March ye 7th.

"He wase borne at Eastnunwell, in ye chaumber over ye parlour, May ye 12 Ano. Dom. 1585, and wase nursed att Borderwood by one Cooke's wyfe in a littel tennement of Baronett Worseleyes : he wase brought up in his infancie at Bewlie (Beaulieu), and afterwards put to schoole at Shalfleete in ye island [1] and Winchester ; from whence he went

Shalfleet Church. By John Fullwood.

to Baylioll College in Oxon, and had a grownde chamber in ye Bach'lor Courte, nexte to a Inne called ye Cateronwheele [the Catharine wheel] . . . After my father's deth I came to live in ye island, and bwylt moost part of ye house [Nunwell]. . . . I was put into ye commission of ye Peace att ye adge of 22 yeres, when I not well understoode myselve or my

---

[1] Shalfleet, near Yarmouth. Its ancient church tower is thought to have been once built for defence. The cost of the spire was paid by selling the metal of the bells and of the parish cannon.

place, and was ashamed to sett on ye Bench, as not hauinge then any hayre on my face and less wit . . . h'e was liftennant Governor of Portsmouth, and was Liftennant of ye island, and lived soom tymes at Chicester, and soomtymes at Nuport. . . . also mutch trobled with a payne in his hedd, which wold last him 2 or 3 days . . . but when he came to 40 yeres that miserable payne left him, and he begann to bee mutch healthier in his bodye than before. But then another infirmitie came to him whych wase greate paynes in ye sowles of his feete. He wase of a midling stature, bigge, but not very fatt ; of a moderate dyott, not caring how littel or how coorse if cleane and handsome : for his intellectual parts let his actions judge of him. God send ye island never a woorse for his paynestaking to administer justice upryghtly to every one . . . He lived at a great rate of expense in his housekepinge, for he alwaies kept 3 servinge men and a footbwoye, besydes retaynors : alwaies his coach well horsed (his coach wase ye second that ever wase on ye island) ; he spent usually £800 every year, soe that he coold not lay up mutch. Of all vices he hated drunkenes ; yet he wold play ye good fellowe, and wold not mutch refrayne from drinkinge 2 or 3 healthes."

The State of " Owre Island" 1627.

"The Isle of Wight, since my memorie, is infinitely decayed, for eythor it is by reason of soe many Attourneys that hathe of late made this theyr habitation . . . or else wanting ye good bargaynes, they [the people] were wont to bye from men of warre, who also vented all oure commodoties att verie high pryces, and readie money was easie to be hadd for all things. Now peace and lawe hath beggared us all, soe that within my memorie manie of ye gentlemen and almost all ye yeomandrie ar undon. . . . .

"I have heard it on tradition, and partly knowe it to be true, that not only heretofore was no lawyer nor attourneye in our island ; but in Sir George Carey's tyme an attourney comynge to settle in ye island, wase, by his commaunde, with a pownd of candels hanging att his breeche, with belles about his legges, hunted owt of ye island ; insoemutch that oure awncestors lived here soe quietly and securelie, beynge neythor troobled to go to London nor Winchester, soe they seldom or never went owt of ye island, insomuch that when they went to London (thinkynge itt an East India voiage), they alwaies made theyre willes, supposing noe trooble lyke to travayle."

The Defences of the Island.

During the war against France, though the Duke of Buckingham made Portsmouth his headquarters, the islanders were persuaded that the

Ryde One Hundred Years ago. From an old print after T. Walmsley.

usual French invasion would be attempted. The island militia were very efficient ; each parish had its field-gun, and from a " trewe noate " of the strength of the island, prepared by Sir John Oglander, it appears that they amounted to 2,000 men, with a Newport band of 300. " Watches and wards, with beacons ready for firing, were kept on all the downs and headlands, and every point and creek was jealously guarded. The watchmen with loaded muskets and lighted matches were changed at sunrise and sunset, and were visited by a 'searcher' twice during the day, and three times at night."[1] Sir John was most eager to have Sandown Castle, then called Sandam Castle, and the other coast defences put in repair, and for the " Isle of Freshwater " to be made a place of refuge. " For my parte, I think ye chardge that by Sir George Carey was bestowed upon Caresbrooke Castel was to no purpose, and I shold be loft on any occasion to mewe myself up there. If that charge had been made at ffreshwater Gate, itt might have made it both invincible, and a brave receptacle for us, and owre cattel, if att any tyme wee should be beaten att ye landinge. I am now indeavouring in these daungerous tymes to see weathor I can willinglie and voluntarily rayse 100 horse in owre island, and to turn all owre fild-pieces into drakes ;[2] what good service we do must be done at ye landinge." Note the spirit and pluck of the islanders in their own defence. Sir John managed to beg a large sum of money from the Government, and a new fort was built at " Sandam." Moreover, his own " owld clerke, Tobye Kempe," who lies buried near his master, was deputed to keep the accounts at two shillings a day ; and soon Sir John had the pleasure of seeing a garrison there.

" Rychard Cooke, of Budbridge, wase a captayne of Sandam Castle, a brave fellow, came always to Arreton Church in his wrought velvet gowne, and 12 of his soldiers with habbardes wayghted upon him."

" *An Egyptian Thraldom.*"

But of trouble there was no end. The king billeted a regiment of 1,000 Scots on the island, and Sir John was nearly worn out before he got rid of them.

" Never entertayn moor sowldiers into youre island, beinge a thinge you maye refuse, and an unsupportable troble and miserye, *espeiiollie Scotchmen*, for I may trulye say, since ye Danes beinge here, theyre never was a greater miserye hapened to us than ye bilitinge of these Lorde-danes. . . . . On ye 3rd of September wee were freed from owre Egiption thraldome or lyke Spane from their Moores."

---

[1] Introduction to extract from the Oglander MS. by Mr. W. H. Long.
[2] Light field guns used as " horse artillery."

Arrested and Sent to London.

In the published extracts of the MS. there is a gap from 1632 to 1647. In the interim Sir John, a good Royalist, was arrested and sent to London to answer before Parliament for a remark that he would give £500 for king to be in possession of the fleet. There is no published part of Sir John's notes dealing with this period. But by the kindness of Mr. John Glynn Oglander, the present owner of Nunwell, I have seen the original warrant which was sent to Colonel Carne to arrest Sir John.

It is written on a small piece of paper, which when folded would go into an ordinary envelope, and runs thus :—

" At the committee of the Lords and Commons for the safety of the Kingdom. These are to pray and authorise you to send up in safe custody to the committee the person of Sir John Oglander, Knight, to answer such matters as at his coming shall be objected to him. These shall be your sufficient warrant. 13 June.

" Signed   (1643).

> " PEMBROKE.
> MONTGOMERY.
> MANCHESTER.
> W. SAY & SEALE.
> H. VANE.
> THOMAS BARRINGTON.
> JO. PYM."

Sir John has treated this document with quiet contumely. In one corner he has scribbled " my warrant," and on the back he has tried a quill pen. But he was heavily fined, his wife died while he was in custody, and his high character and patriotism in regard to the island were ignored wholly.

He entertains the King.

It was in part his known loyalty that induced the king to risk himself in the island. Sir John's account of his arrival is given elsewhere. But he did much to cheer the king in the early days of his confinement at Carisbrooke : entertained him in his house, and presented him with a purse of £1,000 in gold, considerably more than a year's expenses of the knight's household. He was also present at the last speech made by Charles at Newport to the Commissioners, in which he predicted his own fate, before he was seized by the soldiers and deported to London. The king spoke "with mutch cheerfulnesse and a serene countenance, and carridge free from any disturbance ; and then hee p'rted from ye Lordes and Commissioners, leavinge manie tender impressiones, if not in them, in ye other hearers."

Purely Personal.

Much of Sir John's memoranda seems to have been designed for the reading of his own family. He had a very great curiosity and pride in all relating to the personal life of the past Oglanders, and expected his descendants to share this feeling. Perhaps the oddest evidence of this care for the enlightenment of his posterity as to his own personality, next after that in his description of himself, was recently found in a small box, probably the one which is referred to more than once in his MS., in which were a number of very old deeds and papers, tied up by handsome pieces of gold lace, silver lace, and narrow bands of silk, plaited into patterns with colours of green and white, brown and white, or blue and white ; all these laces have silver or gold tags at the end. A note written inside the lid of the box by Sir John explains the mystery :—

"These Quicknesses that are here tyed up weare so done by Sir John Oglander with his owne poynts, every one of them haue been worne by him. And it may bee that in futor tyme somme of his successors may wonder at the fashion. Witness the same, my hand—John Oglander."

The laces are the "points" which laced the trunk hose of the day to the doublet, and in a fine portrait of Sir John in his best velvet suit, he appears wearing a set of silver lace points, with the tags showing all round the waist.

Sir John on his Neighbours.

His greatest friend was Sir Richard Worsley, of Appledurcomb. Sir Richard had lost an eye at Winchester, but was "wonderful studious, insomutch that he affected no counterye spoortes, eyther hawkinge or huntinge, but spent his tyme wholly at his booke when he wase alone ;

verie merry, and a notable good fellowe in companie that he knew. *He delighted much in flinging of cuschions at one another's heddes only in sporte and for exercise;* until that with a cuschion at Gatcombe I was lyke to put out his other eye."

Sir Richard Worsley was buried with his daughter at the fine church

Carved Tombstones and Dial, Godshill.   By R. Serle.

at Godshill, in the centre of the island.   "She was buryed," writes Sir John, "by her father in ye chauncel at Godshill Church, where sutch a father, sutch a daughter lyeth ; both sutch as I must confess I never knewe any that exceeded them."

A Bad Neighbour.

" Mr. Robert Dyllington was the sonn of one Goddardes daughter, a merchaunt in Hampton, after whose base and miserable conditions he mutch tooke, insomutch that his unkell, Sir Robert, could hardly endure him.

" Marrying with a woman lyke himself, they grew soe miserably base, as in one instance for all, when Anie came to his house with horses he hath often been found in ye rack and manger takinge awaie the haye ; but by these thrifty coorses, from one of ye meanest in ye island, he grew soe ritch as he purchased Motson of Mr. Cheke." Sir John at last "sent him one who had a Baronnetship to sell," which he bought cheap, and " is nowe inferior to none."

Another Way to Grow Rich.

" Mr. Emanuel Badd was a verie poor man's sonn, and bound apprentice to one Bernard, a shoomaker of Nuport. But by God's blessing and ye loss of 5 wives he grewe very ritch, pourchased ye Priory (St. Helen's Priory) and mutch other lands in ye island."

Sir John lies buried in the Oglander chapel, in the beautiful church at Brading.

Even his monument is of no common kind. It is an effigy of life-size, clad in complete armour, carved in wood, and painted of the natural colours. The modelling of the hands and face is very lifelike—the veins showing, the brow slightly furrowed, the eyes open and dark, as is the hair and moustache. Above him, in a niche, lies a tiny effigy of his favourite son George, who died at the age of twenty-three, and opposite is a monument to his father, Sir William Oglander.

The following touching entry in his notes refers to the death of his favourite son :—

" Wooldest thou know wheather Sir John Oglander had an elder son than William ? I resolve thee he had : his name was George, after his grandfather Moores [1] name. And I tell ye he was sutch a sonn as ye Isle of Wight never bredd ye lyke before, nor ever will ye lyke agayne. *Periendo, Perio.* O George, my son George, thou wast to goode for

[1] Sir George Moore, of Losely, near Guildford.

mee, all partes naturol and artificioll did soe abound in thee, that hadst
thou lived, thou hadst been an honour to thy family and thy countery.
But thou art dedd, and with thee all my hopes. *Vale, Vale, tempore
sequor.*"

The fine church is all that is left of the glories of Brading, which once
stood at the head of Brading Haven. Now it is left at two miles distance
from the sea by the reclamation of its harbour. The town still preserves
its parish stocks and a tiny town hall, probably the smallest in England,
and a bull-ring, with the large iron ring to which the bull was fastened
when baited.

Even in the time of the Commonwealth it was much decayed.
"Bradinge in Queen Elizabeth's tyme wase a handsome towne," writes
Sir John Oglander. "There weare in itt many good liviers that myght
dispence £40 a yeare a peece, now not one."

From Brading town to St. Helen's stretched until recently the wide
estuary of Brading Haven. Now, with the exception of enough to make
a useful harbour at Bembridge, this great estuary, where Sir John
Oglander's father would shoot "forty fowl of a night," has been
reclaimed by the directors of the "Liberator" Companies.

The nature of the appeal made by this wild scheme in the first
instance to the daring speculators who, seventeen years ago, embarked the
resources of the company in an enterprise of which not only the practical
difficulty, but the financial worthlessness, had already been proved by
actual experiment, as early as the reign of James I., will probably remain
among the unknown factors of commercial failure. The belief in the
possibility of getting "Something for nothing," due to the notion that
land won from the sea is a kind of treasure-trove, may have quieted the
first misgivings of shareholders. But the fact that Sir Hugh Myddelton,
the engineer of the New River, though a "crafty fox and subtle citizen,"
as Sir Oglander noted, had ultimately failed, not only to maintain his
reclamation of Brading Haven, but to make it pay while the dam lasted,
was well known in the history of engineering ; and though the mechanical
difficulties might be overcome by modern machinery, the nature of the
harbour bottom for the growth or non-growth of crops and grasses could
hardly have changed. Briefly, the past history of the Brading reclamation
was as follows. In 1620 Sir Hugh Myddelton dammed the mouth of

the river Yar at Bembridge, opposite Spithead, and on the seven hundred acres of land so reclaimed he "tried all experiments in it ; he sowed wheat, barley, oats, cabbage-seed, and last of all rape-seed, which proved best ; but all the others came to nothing." "The nature of the ground, after it was inned," wrote Sir John Oglander, "was not answerable to what was expected, for almost the moiety of it next to the sea was a light, running sand, and of little worth. The inconvenience was in it, that the sea brought so much sand and ooze and seaweed that these choked up the passage for the water to go out, insomuch that I am of opinion that if the sea had not broke in there would have been no current left for the water to go out, so that in time it would have laid to the sea, or else the sea would have drowned the whole country. Therefore, in my opinion, it is not good meddling with a haven so near the main ocean."

This experiment had cost in all £7,000, when the sea broke in ten years later, and Sir Hugh Myddelton's fields once more became harbour-bottom, and cockles and winkles once more grew where his meagre crops of oats and rape had struggled for existence. Some years later an offer was made to repair the dam for £4,400, but this fell through. No one thought it worth while to spend the money, though small arms and creeks of the harbour were from time to time banked off and reclaimed by adjacent landowners. The attempt which had baffled Sir Hugh Myddelton was suddenly revived by the Liberator directors seventeen years ago. The sea was banked out, almost on the lines of Sir Hugh Myddelton's dam, a straight channel of double the size necessary for the mere drainage of the higher levels was cut for the passage of the river and the holding of its waters during high-tide, when the sluices are automatically closed ; and a railway and quay were added, with a hotel at Bembridge. Solid and costly as their embankment was, the sea broke in, steam-engines and machinery were toppled from the dykes and buried in the mud, workmen were drowned, and the whole enterprise was within an ace of becoming a little Panama. But at last the sea was beaten, 643 acres of weltering mud were left above water, and the reclamation, such as it is, is probably won for ever. But at what a cost ! Four hundred and twenty thousand pounds are debited to the Brading reclamation, of which vast sum we may assume that £100,000 were expended on the railway quay and buildings, leaving £320,000 as the price of 643 acres of sea-bottom.

As reclamation of mud-flats and foreshores has lately been much advocated as a means of providing "work and wages," and of adding to the resources of the country, the present state and probable future of the land won from the sea at Brading is a matter of some interest, omitting all considerations of the original cost. We may concede at once that, from the picturesque point of view, the reclaimed harbour is a great

Brading Haven.   By John Fullwood.

improvement on the ancient mud-flats. It has added to the Isle of Wight what seems a piece of Holland, covered with green pasture and grazing cattle. This area is as much withdrawn from the intrusion of man as the old lagoon ; for as on the mud-flats there were no roads, no rights-of-way, and no footpaths, so the reclamation is a roadless district, secured absolutely to the use of the occupiers, and incidentally to the wild-fowl which swarm by its shallow pools and drains. The broad embanked river runs straight through the centre, and divides into two the level which lies like a green sea between the ring of surrounding hills and the harbour-bank. In this river, the waters of the ancient reclamations higher up the valley collect during high-water, when the pressure from the sea automatically shuts the sluices, and pour out during low-tide, when the pressure of the sea is removed, through the iron gates, near which lie, with the grooves still sound and sharply cut, parts of the sluices made for Sir Hugh Myddelton of English oak in the year 1621. The general shape of the reclamation is an oval, with one of the smaller ends facing the sea and the other abutting on ancient dams near Brading, two miles higher up the valley. The whole of this has been converted into firm, dry land ; neither is its quality so inferior as Sir Hugh Myddelton judged. Possibly the improvement in the seventeen years during which the old sea-bottom has been exposed to sun and rain, has been proportionately more rapid than in the ten in which it was exposed to the air after 1620. Then half the area was described as consisting of " light, running sand of little worth," though the upper portion promised to become valuable pasture. Those advocates of reclamation of land from the sea, who propose to " leave it to Nature " when the sea has once been barred out, can see at Brading and Bembridge what it is exactly that Nature does, and how far art can help to make old sea-bottom into pasture for cattle, and even into a playground for men and women, in seventeen years. It must be remembered that in this case Nature has been hurried, and made to do her work before her time. Left to itself, the harbour would have silted up in the course of centuries, and the pastures would have grown of themselves on land already covered with the alluvial mould. As it is, the sea was swept from the land, which had to take its chance as it was—mud, sand, shingle, or cockle-beds, just as they came. There was not even an earthworm on the whole six hundred acres to move the soil and help the rain to wash the salt out of it. The wonder is not that the change has taken place so slowly, but that the change from a soil supporting marine vegetable growth to a soil largely covered with grass, clover, and trefoil, has matured so quickly. What was once the head of the bay is now good pasture covered with cattle and letting for 30s. an acre—there are one hundred and fifty acres of this good ground. Nature had already prepared it in part—for it was mud washed from the valley above—and still preserves in contour, though covered with grass, the creeks and " fleets " in which the tide rose and fell. All round the fringes of the flat, where it joins the old shore, the

E

earthworms have descended and made a border of fair soil. On one side sewage has been run into the hungrier soil, and there, on a natural level, the true use and place of such experiments is seen. Three crops of grass a year are cut from ground which otherwise would not fetch more than 5s. an acre—a hint, perhaps, for the disposal of some of the London "effluent." There remains a portion of dead, sour greensand on which no herbage grows, though the advance of soil and grass may be noted, like the gradual spread of lichen on a tree. Each patch of rushes, each weed and plantain, gathers a little soil round its roots or leaves, and the oasis spreads until all is joined and made one with the better ground. A cattle-farm and nursery garden occupy the centre of the seaward curve. The farm is already surrounded by rich grasses, clover, and sweet herbage, and the garden is a wonder of fertility. Not only vegetables, but roses, chrysanthemums, carnations, lavender, and other garden flowers are there reared in profusion; and in the winter masses of mauve veronica are in blossom. In walking over what is now good pasture, the evidences of the recent nature of all this agricultural fertility crop up on every side. Where the turf lies in knolls and hillocks, the sea-shells may still be seen lying bleached or purple among the roots of the grass, and what would be taken for snail-shells elsewhere are found to be little clusters of the periwinkles and mussels for which Brading Haven was once famous. But perhaps the greatest success in the conversion of the old harbour to daily use is the present condition of the "light, running sand" near the sea. This sand must have a stratum of clay beneath it, for groves of poplar trees planted on it are now in vigorous growth. But for some years the land lay barely covered with cup-moss, lichen, and thin, poor grass, a haunt of rabbits and shore-birds. It is now converted into a golf-ground, and studded at short intervals with level lawns of fine turf for "putting greens," which daily extend their area, and promise before long to convert the "running sands" into a beautiful and park-like recreation ground. The beauty of the whole scene is much increased by the number of half-wild swans, which are constantly in movement, either swimming upon the pools and streams, or flying to and from the sea. These swans are among the natural agents busied in aiding the reclamation of the land. They feed almost entirely upon the weeds which would otherwise choke up the dykes, and it is believed that two

Sundown. Bay.

swans do as much work in keeping the waterways free and open as could be done by a paid labourer.

The history and fortunes of a given area of land are the constant subject of story. The rise and fall of the importance of a particular part of the sea, except perhaps as constituting a fishery, has seldom been made the theme of a historian. Yet there are certain areas of sea off the English coasts which have an average population much greater than that of the adjacent land, and have maintained this pre-eminence for centuries. There are the great roadsteads off the English coasts, places in which ships and their crews congregate as naturally for food, shelter, or refit, as do the sea-fowl off certain parts of the coast. The proximity of a great harbour is not a necessary feature of such roadsteads. The fleets of vessels which in certain winds lie off the " Downs " in the Channel have little or no communication with the shore. But usually the roadstead lies off a harbour, and the permanence of the port makes the occupation of the adjacent sea a matter of course, so long as the harbour continues to be used. For some reason this has not been the case at Portsmouth and Spithead.

St. Helen's Roads, off St. Helen's Point, and opposite the mouth of the old Brading Haven, now Bembridge Harbour, was once the favourite anchoring ground of the British fleets when about to leave for foreign service ; and their communications with the island were almost as frequent and important as with Portsmouth itself. The fleets used to leave Spithead and anchor off St. Helen's, sending to Bembridge, at the point where a spring of fresh water runs down from the sloping cliff to the sea, to fill their water casks, and to the little village of Bembridge itself for their fresh meat, so long as they remained, which was taken out daily to the ships in " row-barges." Hence the old inn was originally called the " Row-Barge ; " and the country people, farmers, and village tradesfolk profited greatly by the presence of the fleet. For a time the Isle of Wight held the place for which it seemed naturally suited in those days, of a victualling-ground for the minor needs of the fleet. Sir John Oglander, long before this, had foreseen this possibility, though he did not expect the development which brought the ships to the mouth of the harbour which lay almost in touch with his own park at Nunwell. He proposed that a new port and road should be

E 2

made at Cowes for a "rendezvous." "If the country would have so
much discretion as to make good use of that harbour, as first to have an
honest man to be captain there, to build storehouses, to have by a joint
store of all provision, and to have that their rendezvous, and to victuall
there, they need no other market nor means to make the island happy
and fortunate."

The first account of a British fleet lying for a long period off St.
Helen's is preserved in the Fleming Collection at Rydal Hall, and gives
the list of ships and "order of array" for an expected battle with the
French in 1545. Henry VIII., only two years before his death, drifted
into war with both France and Scotland on the burning question of
the betrothal of the baby princess, Mary Queen of Scots, to Edward
the Prince of Wales. Henry was at that time in the position of a
tenant for life of a large estate, who has exhausted the savings of his
ancestors and his own credit. He had only two more years to live, but
the national, or rather the royal, exchequer was drained. All his father's
savings were spent. The whole of the Church property had already been
sold in the greatest possible hurry at the lowest possible price. The last
financial expedient of debasing the coinage till the proportion of base
metal was as four to six, had brought nothing in, and destroyed credit ;
and Henry, in his old age, found himself threatened with a French
invasion, and without means to equip a sufficient fleet.

The Isle of Wight was, as usual, marked for one of the first objectives
of the French. The people were warned, the watch-fires laid, Carisbrook
Castle victualled and armed, and a fleet, partly equipped from England
and partly, as it would seem, hired from the Baltic, was stationed in St.
Helen's Roads as a partial protection. The following quaint document
gives the list of ships, with indications of the place from which the
foreign vessels were hired. It did not amount to more than 100 sail,
whereas the French had 200, besides galleys.

"A.D. 1545. Orders concerning the fleet. Thes be the shepes
apoynted for the furste front of the wauntiguard [vanguard].

"In primes. The *Great Arragosea* [? the Mary Rose], the *Sampson
Lubyke,*[1] the *Trenyte* of Danske [Trinity of Dantzic], the *Mary* of

---

[1] *Lubyke* signifies that the ship came from Lubeck ; *Danske* = of Dantzic ; *Hanbrake*
= of Hamburg.

Hanbrake, the *Pelicane*, the *Murryan* [the Mary Anne], the *Sepiar* of Nanske.

"The second rancke of the vauntward :—The *Harry-Gracy-a-adewe* [This name was evidently a severe trial to the spelling of the naval officer who drew up the memorandum. He means the *Harry, Grace à Dieu*, Henry VIII.'s largest battleship.] The *Venichean* [Venetian], the *Peter Pomygarnate* [Pomegranate], the *Pansys*, the *Greate Galley*, the *Swepstacke*, the *Mennyon* [the Minion], the *Sallow*, the *New Barke*, the *Saule Argaly*.

"The iij rancke of the vauntward :—The *Berste Denar* [what can this mean?] the *Facon Lyfelay*, the *Harry Brestow* [of Bristol], the *Trenyte Rynnegar* [?] the *Mary Jeames* [Mary James], the *Pelgrim* of Dartmouthe, the *Mary Gorge* of Rye [Mary George of Rye], the *Thomas Topkynes* [Thomas Tompkins], the *Jhorges Breyges* [George Brydges], the *Ane Lyfelay* [Anne Lively], the *Jhon the Evangeleste*, the *Thomas Madely*, the *Lartyche*, the *Crystofer Tennet*, the *Mary Fortune*, the *Mary Marten*, the *Trenytye Brestow*."

"Galleys and shepes" on the right and left wings were also named for service, including even pinnaces from the Baltic—the "Runygar pinnes" looks like an attempt at "Reinecke," and is clearly German— down to "iij botes of Rye."

This "scratch" fleet was all the protection on which the islanders could count besides their new forts, some of which were not completed, and the English Admiral, who seems to have had the proper instinct as to the value of a "fleet in being" for the protection of the country from invasion by sea, resolved to do exactly what Admiral Colomb and Captain Mahan have concluded was the right course under such circumstances—to keep his fleet in observation off St. Helen's, where it was fairly protected by the sands and shoals; just as Lord Torrington proposed to do when a superior French fleet threatened the Isle of Wight when William III. was away fighting the rebels in Ireland.[1] Lord Torrington was forced to fight, and be beaten, by the imperative orders of the Queen. Apparently Henry VIII.'s admiral was also pressed by superior authority to fight, and lose the advantage which

[1] Torrington was lying in St. Helen's Roads when the news came that the French fleet was anchored in Freshwater Bay.

a masterly inaction would have secured.   The order of the fleet given above was made in pursuance of a decision to force a battle " which, upon the King's determination, should be on Monday, the 10th of August."

If the fleets had been equal in numbers, and the fate of the island in no way concerned, the directions for manœuvres during the engagement might have commended themselves.   Under the circumstances though, they are an interesting evidence of the very modern character of the seamanship of the day ; they seem based on the assumption that the fleets were even in numbers, though the French force was double that of the English.

The instructions given were most precise ; there was to be half a cable length between the ships.   The front rank (" the wauntigarde ") was to make sail straight to the front of the battle, pass through, and make a short return to the centre, having special regard to the course of the second rank.   The ships of the second and third ranks were to lay aboard the principal ships of the enemy, the *Admiral* being reserved for my Lord Admiral.

Every ship of the first rank was to carry a St. George's Cross upon the foretopmast during the fight.   Those in the second rank were to carry one upon the main mast, and those in the third rank on the " messel maste top " (mizzen top).   The wings were to wait and observe the issue of the battle, and "give succour as they shall see occasion."

Probably the Admiral thought he knew his business better than the king's advisers at Whitehall, for he did not fight any such battle as was sketched in the instructions.   He remained in St. Helen's Roads, until the arrival of the French fleet of two hundred sail, and then engaged them partially in the hope of getting them entangled in dangerous waters.   The cannonading lasted for two days, and the *Mary Rose* was sunk.   It seems evident that the English were driven from St. Helen's, and that the French were for some time off the island, and able to make partial descents.

In the great war at the end of the last century, St. Helen's Roads were in 1797 the scene of what is known to history as the "Mutiny at Spithead." [1]   The first refusal of the crews of the fleet to sail was

---

[1] See an interesting account read by Mr. G. Long, before the Portsmouth Literary Society, published in the *Portsmouth Times*, Dec. 2, 1893.

after the order to leave Spithead. But after the Admiralty had made certain concessions, the fleet weighed and anchored at St. Helen's. There the mutiny broke out afresh. Every ship refused to sail, when Lord Bridport made the signal to leave for Brest, because the Admiralty had taken no steps to fulfil their promises. The " delegates " assembled, and proceeded to the *London,* Admiral Colpoys's ship, with the intention of holding their convention there. The Admiral ordered them to sheer off, which they refused to do. He then ordered the marines to fire into the boats, which they did, killing five men and wounding six. On this becoming known, the seamen rushed in crowds up the hatchways, overpowered the officers, and disarmed the marines. They then seized the first lieutenant, Mr. Peter Boven, who had shot and killed a seaman who had unlashed one of the guns and was proceeding to turn it on the quarter-deck. Admiral Colpoys then took the full responsibility on himself, and, fully expecting to be hanged by the mutineers, made his will and wrote a final letter to Lord Howe explaining what had happened. The seamen, however, delivered him up to the Mayor of Portsmouth for a civil trial !

It was not until the arrival of Lord Howe at St. Helen's, with the fullest assurances that all promises made by the Government should be fulfilled, and that all the mutineers would be pardoned, that the crews returned to order and obedience.

The gain to the health of the neighbourhood, which Sir John Oglander observed was the result of the few years' reclamation of Brading Haven in his day, and which must be even more marked after the permanent reclamation of the mudflats now effected, has not caused any loss of beauty in the existing harbour of Bembridge. The bright, clear waters are no longer a mere covering for weltering mud exposed during the greater part of every tide. The curving dyke, quay, and pier, which form the defence of the reclamation are washed by deep water. The harbour runs back some distance inland so as to form a miniature lake, and is the head-quarters of that modern and charming development of yachting, in which the owner manages and sails his own boat. The harbour looks like a basin specially built to hold these pretty little toys, which in rough weather can be raced round the inner waters, and at other times sail out boldly into the Solent or towards the open Channel.

A recent development of this small yacht racing awards the prize entirely to skill in seamanship—apart from the inevitable accidents of wind or tide. A club owns a number of sailing boats of identical build and rig. The members thus start even, so far as the ship is concerned, and the contest resolves itself into a friendly rivalry in the art of sailing and steering.

A dozen of these boats, with their yellow, tanned sails, dancing over the waters towards the fort on the sand spit, or racing round the harbour while the waves are toppling outside, form a new and dainty feature in the harbour landscape. At the head of the new haven is an ancient tide-mill. This is worked by the outflow of water carried into two very large ponds at high tide. It was originally built by Sir Hugh Myddelton, and is still worked, but the size of the small lakes necessary to accumulate enough water to drive the wheel after the ebb has begun to flow raises doubts whether the use of " tidal energy " is ever likely to be a financial success. But the old mill is a picturesque object at the head of the harbour ; there the swans assemble to eat the grain which may have fallen into the water where the sacks are unloaded ; and the cormorants at high tide dive almost beneath its walls in search of the eels which make their way towards the in-fall of the fresh stream. As the tide ebbs they fly out to sit on the buoys which mark the entrance to the harbour, and at the same time the swans which are feeding inland in the reclaimed portion of the haven take wing and fly in pairs, or even in larger numbers, over the harbour out to sea.

The sight and sound of the swans in flight is one of the most picturesque accompaniments of a sail in Bembridge harbour. They fly with rapid beats of the wing, high enough to clear the masts of both yachts and country craft in the basin, each stroke of their wings producing a musical, ringing sound, something like that of a tubular bell.

If the rest of the island disappeared, the " Isle de Bembridge " as it is called on the excellent old maps which were made in France with a view to its invasion and conquest, would still give a very accurate idea of the general character of the whole of " the Wight." It has its harbour and estuary, its river, rising close to the southern shore, like the western " Yar," and running northwards toward the Solent, and in

its land contour presents all the typical features of the island. Near
the harbour mouth the low cliff is covered with trees almost to where
the pebbles touch its foot, and the pretty houses look on the blue
sea set between groves of Mediterranean pines. The eastern point,
called the Foreland, rises above a long and dangerous reef of black
rocks called Bembridge Ledge. But the fields are cultivated to the
very edge of the sea, and " Foreland Farm " with its tall elms, com-
fortable barns, stables and cow-houses, and carefully tilled arable fields
sown with the usual root and corn crops to the brow of the cliff,
is no more modified in its appearance and management than if it
stood in the centre of the island. At the back of the Bembridge
peninsula are White Cliff Bay, another and not less beautiful Alum
Bay, and the splendid ridge of Bembridge Down running, just as
Freshwater Down does, parallel to the sea, with its southern side scarped
into an immense precipice of glittering chalk.

Until recently there was not a single house visible from Whitecliff
Bay, and at present the number is limited to a single building, much
beaten by winter storms. The cliffs of this beautiful semicircle corre-
spond in their general order to those of Alum Bay ; but the clay slopes
to the left and centre are firmer, steeper, and covered with a rich growth
of golden grass, brambles, flowers, and waving " mare's tail," and in
other places with masses of blackthorn, and beds of scarlet and yellow
osiers. The bright coloured sands which lie between the clay and the
chalk are less brilliant and show fewer colours than those at Alum Bay.
The vertical strata are also thicker, and stand in peaked scarps, between
each of which and the next is a " chine " deep in bracken and set with
flowers. The point corresponding to that which in Alum Bay ends in
the Needle Rocks, is at Whitecliff Bay an abrupt precipice of chalk, with
a submarine reef jutting from its foot. This precipice closes the bay,
and is the pillar which marks the eastern approach between sea and
crag to the foot of the Culver Cliff.

Though not so lofty as those at Freshwater, it is equally beautiful,
whether seen from above, where a narrow path goes down to a cave,
called the Hermit's Hole, or from its foot where the retreating tide
leaves space enough to stand below, and look up to the summit. The
different exposure of the chalk alters its character at each succeeding

bastion. In some it is so smooth as not to give a hold even to the creeping samphire ; in others the juts and ledges are covered by. plants and lichens, and haunted by nesting gulls and cormorants. Every year the raven and the peregrine falcon make their eyrie in the Culver Cliff. The birds may be seen on any day throughout the year, never leaving the cliff face for any length of time, and often rearing their young in spite of the cragsmen.

The antiquity of this peregrine eyrie can be proved by documents.

The Manor House, Yaverland. By John Fullwood.

In June 1564, Queen Elizabeth issued a warrant to Sir Richard Worsley, Captain of the Isle of Wight, to search for hawks stolen from the Queen's land in the island, and for committing to ward and examining the " malefactors," who had been faulty of this "stealth and presumtuous attempt." The warrant, which was issued at Richmond and signed by Lords North, Dudley, Pembroke, Howard, and Sir W.

Cecil—a curious instance of the keenness with which the Tudor sovereigns guarded their rights—does not specify whether the nests robbed were at Culver or Freshwater ; but tradition says the former.   The Culver eyrie supplied falcons to the island gentry in the days of James I., for Mr. George Oglander, " had a lanorett that was bred in ye·White Cliff on Bimbridge, which was ye best hawk with ye worst lookinge to, that wase in England ; for they nevor took care of her, but gave her meat in ye foote, scarce evor tyed her, but lett her scratch for bones with ye dogges ; and when they came afield they cast her off, and she wold followe ye dogges and kill whatsoever did rise, partriche, phesant, bitteron, hearon, hare or coney."   There is no place on the English coast where this rare falcon can be seen so easily as on the White Cliff at Bembridge. The writer has visited it some twenty times, and never missed seeing one or a pair of these representatives of what is perhaps the oldest family remaining in the island.

The beautiful Jacobean manor house of Yaverland stands on the site of what was the ancient home of the Lords, not only of the Manor of Yaverland, but of the Isle of Bembridge, so far as its protection and defence demanded a captain.   It was granted to Sir William Russell, an ancestor of the Duke of Bedford, by Edward I.   There the people of the island used to send the first news of the coming of the French, and the Lords of Yaverland would summon their men and lead the array of the island.   When the French landed at Bembridge in 1340 Sir Theobald Russell, of Yaverland, met them and drove them back to their ships, but was himself killed in the fight.   There is a persistent tradition that the little church which stands by the manor house was built, not on the spot, but at Woolverton a short distance off, on the shore of the ancient Brading Haven.   The local story is that the town of Woolverton was burnt by the French and every person killed but one, before the Knight of Yaverland could come to help them. The site of the old town is well authenticated, and is now covered by a thick wood called the " Centurion's Copse " (St. Urian's Copse according to antiquaries).   The stones of the *Norman* chapel at Woolverton were taken to Yaverland when Sir William Russell built the church at Yaverland for the con- venience of his household.   The road, which anciently ran by Woolver- ton, is now carried higher up the hill-side above, a change made, according to the same tradition, because the ghosts of the dead people of Woolverton haunted the ruins where they made their last stand against the French.

The traces of this ancient town which was strangled out of existence in a night, standing on the shores of a harbour which is now dry land, and called by a name dating from an earlier period than the foundation of the town itself, are a typical example of the history of the island and the sufferings of its inhabitants in its old and evil days.

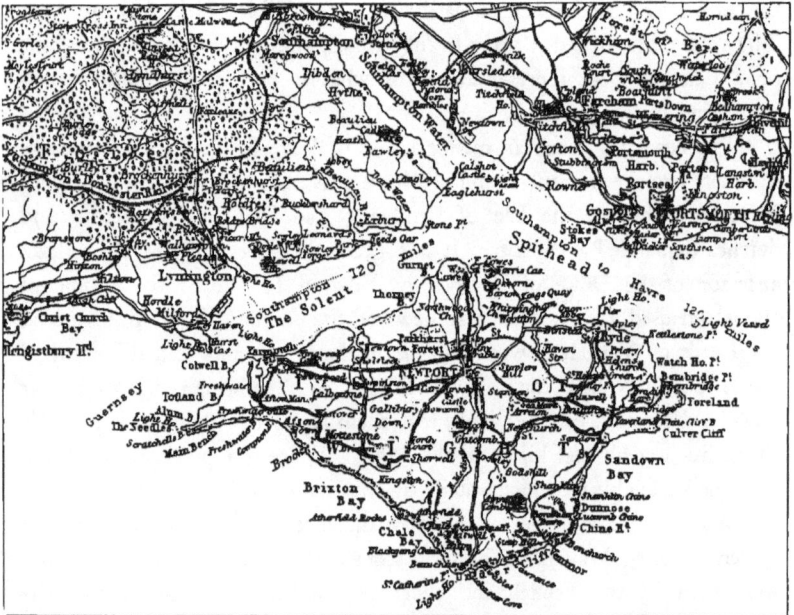

Map of the Isle of Wight.

INDEX

www.ingramcontent.com/pod-product-compliance
Lightning Source LLC
Chambersburg PA
CBHW031451270326
41930CB00007B/950